There Where You Do Not Think To Be Thinking

Views From Tornado Island, Book 12

(from *theforestforthetrees*)

Charles Stein

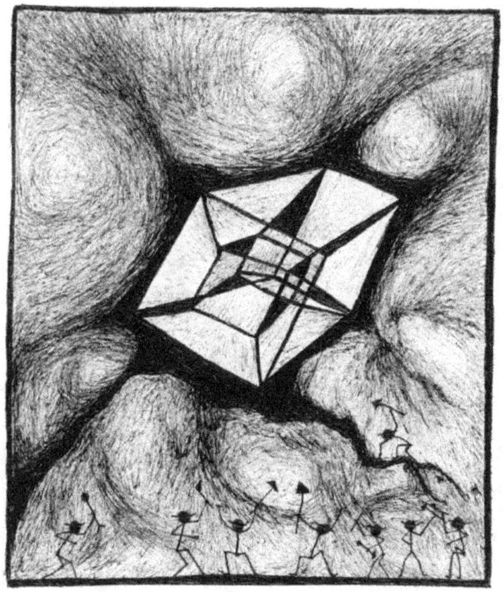

Spuyten Duyvil
New York City

ISBN 978-1-941550-12-0

Library of Congress Cataloging-in-Publication Data

Stein, Charles, 1944-
[Poems. Selections]
There where you do not think to be thinking / Charles Stein.
pages ; cm
ISBN 978-1-941550-12-0
I. Title.
PS3569.T363A6 2014
811'.54—dc23

2014023404

For Nathan Ray Smith and Jenny Fox,
who heard practically everything in the entire series of Books
in Views From Tornado Island *as they were written.*
I am enormously grateful for their attention.

Contents

One: Heredity 1
Two: Stability 9
Three: Volatility 17
Four: Incomprehensibility 23
Five: Absence 31
Six: With Tobacco Woman 39
INTERVAL 46
INTERVAL 48
Seven: Dispersion 49
INTERVAL 57
Eight: Inherit the Globe 59
Nine: A Fine Confusion 67
INTERVAL (for Maximus) 74
Ten: Force Released/Forced Release 81
Eleven: A Pocket Full of Opals 89
Twelve: Hammerhead Rattles his Africas 97
INTERVAL 103
INTERVAL 105
Thirteen: Conjugal Instances 107
INTERVAL 114

GALLERY OF IMAGES 117

Fourteen: World Night, Black Crystal 155
INTERVAL 163
Fifteen: Epistemic Threats 165
Sixteen: Ubiquitous Particulates 175
Seventeen: Money Has An Enemy 185
INTERVAL 191
Eighteen: All The Young Philosophies 193
Nineteen: The Factory 201
Twenty: The Grand Concordat 209
INTERVAL 217

Twenty-One: The Visitor 221
Twenty-Two: Weirdlings and Wastrels 231
Twenty-Three: A Further Report from
Our Visitor with Remarks on Telestics 239
INTERVAL 243
INTERVAL 244
Twenty-Three, continued 245
Twenty-Four: The Cat's Bowl 251
INTERVAL: Elsewhere 258
Twenty-Five: Mind Games 261
Twenty-Six: The Kingdom 271

POSTSCRIPT: The Cryptographic Matrix 277

"You are not *here*
where you are the plaything of your thought,
but *there*
where you do not think to be thinking."

Jacques Lacan

One: Heredity

My Heredity, I say,
is like a Black Box —
a Crystal
in a cloud
above Tornado Island,
a volatile flux of sentient particulates
compressed in such a cloud as such a Crystal.

It is a fragile omen.
The information of it
fluctuates as if
Black Box pocketed Crystal,
a volatile stone
to manifest as Happenstance.

Deep Storage cannot hold it —
a statistical distribution so recondite
that Hammerhead's avatars
in an on-site *excavation* of Deep Storage
shall not have *at* it.

Here, in your Old Hotel,
Deep Storage is exposed to exploration.
But hereditary inquisition,
hereditary dispossession,
returns to that Black Box
which supercedes *all* excavation.

[]

I shake my African Rattle
zooming through rooms and corridors,
long hair streaming behind me,
queering the serenity
of The Old Hotel
and its moribund perennials:
old guests on red lounge chairs,
stewing in the halls.
Where is my Opal?

Shall we find our Heredity in spite of it all
secured in Deep Storage?
Our Syzygy grows languid.
But surely together, she and I,
must resume ancestral Dispossession, old news
regenerate
through such anticipation
as only Black Box can devise.
Surely we shall tune our African Rattles,
not out of Africa only,
and the Old Hotel effect
a clarification of consciousness
through our smoky Opal.
Let us resume the great sonorities,
though African Rattles exasperate the lodgers
whom The Old Hotel so extravagantly accommodates
as there rise
through chinks in the floor boards
intimations of Black Lake.

[]

There seems to be no Syzygy for our Nation,
no hortatory complement.
Wrench Boy exacerbates that.
He cultivates Violets
in concentric orbits
about his smoky Opal
in which, were he there to elicit such a figure —
a phantom to convene
our Collective once again —
She would rise from Deep Storage
with such Strength and Stability
that only "the Higher Happenstance"
(whose august governance winds the fertile torsion
that is Tornado Island)
might allow.

Jaguar rules the night.
Happenstance mirrors Black Lake.
Antithetical reciprocals.

African Rattles are silent
though they stand like sentinel pine trees
about The Old Hotel
flaunting in stillness
an Incomprehensible dispersion
of ambient sonorities,
as if no Volatility
fed Happenstance,
no flame-freckled Melee
worked in recess to prepare
a Nation's awakening.
The thing itself
must dissolve.
America fall into the sea.

[]

Shall Dispersion
pass to the limit?

Shall Great Strength open her mouth?

Confusion
fecundates Wrench Boy.

Black Lake spans so broadly
beneath its own Dispossession.

Wrench Boy shall render Volatile
ideation's Globe
and the torqued light
that is Tornado Island
strike Crystal.

The bounds of Existence are Volatile —
"Another Kind of Nation"
to agitate Happenstance.

[]

If "I" could be anyone —
Ubiquity erupt from Deep Storage;
ubiquitous particulates spark
like so many volatile bobbins wound
across the torpid fog
that is the National Happenstance
bereft of Presence —
Deep Storage a sink
for dissipative forces
leached from the Nation —

Wrench Boy himself configured upon
his own diffragilating Heredity: America.
African Rattles
silent like pine trees;
a Nation without alertness
without fascination,
awaiting no more! no more!

the advent of Crystal.

Two:
Stability

No Stability licit
but that it
reflect Black Lake.

Hammerhead's aflame
with his own Volatility.

He likes it.

Not illicit, He.

Yet Hammerhead hammers on
with distracted Presence,
Black Lake but a blur to Hammerhead;
Volatility a metaphysical conundrum
fascinating to Hammerhead.

[]

Contrive a prospect
in which Strength
is metaphysical.

Call it an Old Hotel:
Hereditary Fortitude,
invisible Valor,
a bed of Black Violets
aglimmer at the gardens
abstract at The Old Hotel.

A Black Globe gyrates inconsolably
in the old resort's Red Chamber.

Licit Stability
rests from Black Lake only.
We repeat that.

Only Black Box,
satisfies that Globe.
In the algebraic sense of "to satisfy."
You remove *the value*
and divert it with Black Box. As:

Confusion "satisfy"
Stability.

[]

At The Old Hotel
Wrench Boy bucks
such destabilization
as is fomented by
a certain unrepentant avatar of Hammerhead.

Black Lake
is no Black Box.

Globe
forks out
Confusion.

Black Box
fitted out
for Black Globe:
our Melee's
bailiwick.

[]

Quite generally: Do "phenomena" exist?
Do they *ache*
through their own
Volatility?

Stability but a glance
from our Jaguar.

Wrench Boy
a figure of restraint
but his finger's a trigger.

Black Box.

Syzygy
hidden.

[]

Stability rigors its own regret:
delivers the Strength appurtenant
to Jaguar.

A woman
in white linen
opens the big cat's jaws.

Her force
charges the faces
and ridges,
the vertices
of Crystal.

Clarifies Opal.

Ramifies Jaguar.

And shall She break the Nation
of its legions,
its helmeted black-Hammerhead goon patrols, its fire-chiefs,
ubiquitous and institutional?

Heredity weasels Hammerheads.

Volatility wreaks
of its own extravagant Stability.

[]

Where Dispersion is tactical,
Jaguar gathers the particulates
scattered in his Opal.

[]

The Old Hotel is a Kind and Quaint Museum
on some days: an amulet configured against
unsalutary Incomprehensibility.

The Kind and Quaint Museum
features a New Glob.
Long River is diverted
into a radical flux
of temporal particulates.

[]

Incomprehensibility
"floats"
The Old Hotel,
on loan from the Bank,
its ancestral avatar.

Volatility quieted
by riverine meanderings.

[]

Hammerhead circulates his hovercrafts, his fire-chiefs,
about Tornado Island.

He's the plaything of
an invisible Syzygy:
his ghostlike love dream,
Stability of affect
suppressed desideratum.

Wrench Boy eyes
the proceedings,
ghostlike about
Tornado Island,
mindlike within
The Old Hotel,
fragile down
in the gorge.

[]

Here, where thoughts
shake out
as if from the gentle susurrus
of a mind-bestudded Rattle out of Africa —
Jaguar takes signals from Wrench Boy
to set himself aprowling
about Tornado Island.

Wrench Boy is watching
for Hammerhead's assault
upon The Incomprehensible.

Volatility sups
on the Strength of lions.

Happenstance expatiates
upon the prospect of Melee.

Strength is an image
of a woman
at the lip of a gorge
dressed in white linen.

Three: Volatility

"If my Volatility never reaches Melee,"
pondered Violet,
"my Ubiquity" — WHO SAID THAT?
"I mean my Absence,"
interrupted Violet,
"disperses
your dream."

The Melee in her mind
wasn't listening.

Violet could handle
her own Ubiquity —
the fact of it,
if not the lexical item,
though her fragile grasp
of Vocabulary
was said to be a thing of the past.

But in a text,
time is like a Globe.
Its Stability
rotates
in synchronous alternation
with a distant Syzygy,
in counter-orbit to another Globe
embracing
Nations of temporality — the Volatility
of one world
complemented
by the Volatility
of the other,
Time Passing
by Time-Not-Yet
recalled, not yet become itself
in the melee of recrudescence or remembrance.

Were it not for Black Lake
the time of any Nation
would be nothing but such a text.

"Africa is all of us.
To be alive
is to exacerbate instrumentalities —
black, gourd-bulb rattles
with cowries incised. Volatility
has been in our embrace
long from the past,
but just now gone Global."

Jaguar was speaking to Violet.
Her volatility fluttered.
Her melee sought Black Lake.
"Our Nation"
(she was thinking periphrastically —
the fact,
not the lexical item)
"hides
its African Rattles.
Only Black Lake can recall our Nation now
and open our vision to Crystal."

[]

The idea of Heredity
began to appear
infected with Globe-like Confusions.

Still, Happenstance
though waxing Volatile,
would not reprove Black Lake
or deliver us up
to a *consummate* Confusion.

I seem to be speaking
as if I were Wisdom's Logothete,
which perhaps I am.
But Black Lake
would portend
a secret Volatility
as anodyne
for the fragile commotion
of one's historical state.

Is Hammerhead not like an Ifrit?
Is Happenstance transcendentally encumbered,
a way-station to The Possible?
Is Wrench Boy not a *principle compensatory*,
thus ever out at the elbows, dazzling and volatile?
Who's talking now?
Some habit
I don
or which dons me — here where I am
a play thing
of deep Incomprehensibility
whose mask is clarity,
though I occupy silent chambers
in The Old Hotel and listen
most profoundly
at Black Lake.
And should my incubations thereat gestate
certain uncanny prolusions
internal to this Nation —
if they do, I hide them
under a cloak
of clear Incomprehensibility,
naked affect masking mask,
face, face.

Long River provides me
with requisite Stability.

The jury is never out
regarding Black Lake.

Violet is dizzy.
That's an exaggeration.
But still she is bemused — her natural state,
sweet Violet.
She is my Syzygy.
I confess it, don't regret it,
in spite of a life-long, para-amorous excursion
so that Black Lake
be all the Strength I require—
Strength suffused with Fragility.

Violet's aura modulates Presence:
she manages Happenstance exquisitely
so that her colors flash across facets of Crystal,
Violet waxing Ubiquitous through Happenstance.

Volatility cannot factitiously be suffused
to the absolute water of Black Lake.

It takes the whole Globe
and the exigencies of a Nation
to coagulate Necessity
as some sort of Destiny.
And yet the whole of Happenstance
can flash in your Opal.

Four: Incomprehensibility

Incomprehensibility
was not easy
for Hammerhead.

It was not enough for him
to negotiate
arrangements with his Syzygy.

Does Long River, for example, have one?

Is Heredity
inherent
in Crystal?

A Syzygy's Long River
is its own Syzygy.

The Presence of a Nation
cannot brook
its own Volatility.

No Nation yet has had
the patience to ripen
within a smoky Opal. Well,
not *this* one anyway.

Incomprehensibility
tautologically
fails to comprehend
its own Incomprehensibility.

Such matters
batter
Hammerhead
and set him obsessing about Crystal.

"How can I work my Opal?" he worries.
"It's all a Black Box to me.
But to hell with the Incomprehensible.
My business is with this Nation
and the rapid degeneration of Happenstance,
oblique to it own Syzygy.
                                        Now,
if we could oggle
its double
as in a great mirror,
the Incomprehensible course
it plummets down
would freeze
into a tranquil Crystal,
the Melee of circumstance
appear in an Opal,
a Black Box no more.
I have assimilated Melee more than once
and I do not rue it."

[]

There was a dark smoky Opal
floating about the steel hammer
clutched in the right hand of Hammerhead.
He was wielding the latter
with some menace,
mitigated only
in that he seemed distracted
with a new string
of portentous observations:

"Ubiquitous Presence
is fragile Presence,"

speculated Hammerhead.

"Now, Presence
in the manner of Jaguar,
on the other hand,
or as Long River. . ."

(He was talking about somebody else — a good sign.)

"That would be matter
for profitable discourse,
tracking Presence.

"Ubiquity
is the Mother
of Incomprehensibility. I get that.
But I'll save my Strength for a night
of African Rattles. A Nation
must exceed
mere Happenstance,
Africa in ruins
come back rattling
through Melee.
Shall I call an assembly
in The Old Hotel
to circumvent
by concerted intervention
the inadvertence
of the Volatile
and illuminate
the Occultation
of The Syzygy?"

Violet offered herself
to assist in this operation.
She scattered her seeds on the banks of every long river.
Is she not the Syzygy of all of us?
The GREAT Sygyzy?
To consort with *that*
overwhelms all Fragility.

[]

The Syzygy that doubles the whole world —
her shadow is ubiquitous.
Her Strength knows the force
of ten-thousand Hammerheads.
Her Volatility is organized in her Strength.
She is the Long River
that rushes away
all unsalutary Confusion.

In The Greater Holy Assembly
Volatility is accommodated,
Black Lake compensated,
by local Incomprehensibility.

[]

You cannot *ruin* The Globe.
If the Volatility of a universal population is excited,
incomprehensible as that might be,
Metastability staves off The Nation.
No governance maintains it.
Its African Rattles rally its Strength.
Incomprehensible according to *whom,* might I postulate?
Unsalutary in relation to *what?*
A Melee of African Rattles,
the sounds of shifting oceans.

Melee *requires* the Incomprehensible.
It ratifies her Presence and mien.

[]

Syzygy herself stepped forth
to disperse the occasion
in the form of Jaguar, black and handsome,
as big as the sky.

When is this?

Melee took cover
under
her own Incomprehensibility.

She was a syzygy for Wrench boy.

Five:
Absence

Absence swept Hammerhead away.

Where'd he go?

Wrench Boy
showed up
out of nowhere.

(Feynman diagram to constrain this: the one fellow
was excerpted,
the other recrudesced
together
with a flash of light.)

Vanishing outright
was just too much:

When Wrench Boy materialized,
The Old Hotel was under renovation
bottom to top.

Weird little mountains
poked over the tarmac.

Wrench Boy was about to begin
an illuminating inquiry. Accordingly
he had put on his shoulders
in place of his head
a proper ball of flame,
casting luminous particulates,
sparking traces through a cloud about him
which distributed themselves like star points
in a smoky Opal.

That "civil order" versus "autonomous liberty"
had established itself
as a weighty issue
of social probity,
was frankly Incomprehensible to him.
"Light-thought should flood out all binaries,"
he opined.

"Subcommandante Jaguar," he demanded,
"I summon you to my Opal
black and miasmatical!"

Would Jaguar think it a joke
or slink away in Confusion?
Would the big cat know that that Opal
rendered Ubiquity emblematical,
or consider it an instrument of Absence
since Hammerhead had vanished in a flash?

Of course the smoky bauble
was an avatar of Crystal,
all Confusion resolved,
if submerged in Black Lake. Ubiquity
has no *sense* but as a power
inherent to an Opal
with its data source at Everywhere. Strength herself
was closeted
behind the silky smoothness of its chromatism.

Wrench Boy
was *functionally* Ubiquitous.
He knew from whence he might recover
Hammerhead, if he needed him.

Crystal sat at the center
of his star-bulb head
fielding whatever zoological Confusion
Existence detached from Black Lake —
it was a sidelong glance,
just a casual reference,
struck up by a glint from the Crystal that inspired it:
Crystal fielded Confusion
and deflected it
with a reference to Violet.

[]

Syzygy is no binary
vis à vis Fragility.
They conjugate in Crystal
vis à vis Black Box.

Wrench Boy was satisfied
with Jaguar's oblique response.
He blinked thrice
and held his color.

Thus Wrench Boy computed Existence
as Long River
summoning mud-clods from Ubiquity.

Fragility is no binary
with Strength.

They occupy indifferent
compartments of Black Box.

Black crystals
sprout
from Deep Storage.

[]

Hammerhead has one hammer
made out of Crystal,
one African Rattle
allocated to one Globe.

Incomprehensibility is Crystal's reciprocal.
When she abides in The Old Hotel
she distributes particulates
to whomsoever Wrench Boy
indicates.

Hereditary transport
guides Happenstance.

Wrench Boy
has an eye
on The Nation.

[]

The Old Hotel is ubiquitous.
It happens in a flash.
Wrench Boy claps two wrenches.
What vanishes?

Happenstance, in this instance,
dismisses its universal property.

There are many levels
to appearances
that flash up
in an Opal.

"You can use Volatility — if you're quick,"
instructed Wrench Boy.
"All the force
The Old Hotel commands
taken together
in one grand prospect:
you think you are God, or *a* god,
and are,
except for the Melee,
the incomprehensible torrent
of Long River."

[]

"Not every Ariete and Charlotta
cares to think things through, you know,
so you can *shove* your Feynman diagrams."
Who thought that?

If The Old Hotel is a Melee of Incomprehensibility:
if you displace your Tornado
from the center of *its* "property,"
it just dissolves in the summer heat,
and your obsession with clarity
fades away
to Deep Storage, possibly.
It's Absence is not felt at all
as a quivering sort of Presence.
You might pick up your Opal,
if you've a mind to,
or let it sit where it is
in its own Black Box.

"Opal is a person too, you know," said Violet.

Crystal thought:

"If Happenstance is impertinent,"
(she was gloating about this),
"no Fragility at all
can beset the abstract focus of my facets.
If Black Box is a black box,
The Incomprehensible will change
African Rattle
to an avatar
of some other locality, Peru perhaps;
and crystal spicules precipitate
at unanticipatable junctures
among the filament-like sonorities
of a Rattle out of Anywhere."

[]

Every ceremony
ends with an Opal,
smoky and barely
comprehensible
but smiling with intelligence in quietude
like a Long River.

Six:
With Tobacco Woman

Long River
never
runs out
of
twists and turns

except, perhaps, about Tornado Island
where torque
is at
the limit
and gargantuan violets
violate species parameters
and Jaguar attitudes
go global.

Jaguar
is contemplating
the diversification of his quasi-attributes.

"I ought to be
at least as
volatile as Violet,"
purred Jaguar, "Black,
tan, green, roseate, golden.
I'll saturate a globe
with emblematical variety —
every sub-species jaguar inheriting
a certain confusion of
shall we call it 'cast'? —
my apparent dynamical incoherence
compensating my Ubiquity.
Happenstance shall be suspended for this working
or rather, Confusion make Happenstance my mask.
Diversified too shall be our rattles—
not out of Africa only. Peru, perhaps.
We ourselves are not confused, how should we be?

But Long River runs in a ring
then fans out and becomes
'The Most Asymmetrical Spiral,'
at which point geometry itself
breaks into incommensurate particulates
and reconvenes
in a novel combine
of extravagant principles.
Logic itself is affected in this.
The new geometry breaks
the pigeonholes of Deep Storage.
At every *point* in it
the information modifies its own algorithm
twisting in an agony of defiance
against the very *principle* of the algorithm —
too many species of violet;
too any avatars of Hammerhead;
rattles that grapple toward pure Obliquity and propagate Melee;
Long Rivers that run through Confusion;
ontologies brewed in the vats of Tornado Island;
a crescendo of violets infinitely proliferating,
gigantic and nano-metrical, saturating Possibility Space,
crossing the Great Abyss to The House of Choronzon!
At all events, all of this
is but preparation for The Working
for which I require new humans."

[]

Hammerhead wasn't listening.
He was collecting shapaca leaves
to build Peruvian rattles,
rolling Mapacho stogies.

Melee for Hammerhead
had nothing geometrical about her.
She concentrated her rattles from Anywhere
until she configure her Syzygy.

[]

Now there manifested
an Old Hotel at which
hereditary information
scattered erratically
among its many metamorphic chambers:
One moment, one epoch, one world?
But each inheriting some unanticipatable
element from another
world
not necessarily at all
anterior to it.
But information jagged in from some Elsewhere,
impossible to elucidate.

[]

If you meet your Syzygy
concretely,
Heredity is moot,
exhausted by the crystalline presence
into which the syzygetical energy
collocates ubiquitous
hints and traces
of your infinitely variable and internally diverted presences
from "all around the globe," like they say:
you are distributed in irregular geometries
so that Confusion besets the sub-moieties
of the "tribe" that is your "nature."

Kinship semantics no longer being possible,
the totality of the species amasses
in a Glob of randomly gesticulating particulates.
You are a Nation,
but one whose ubiquitous sovereignty depends on this:
You suck tobacco paste
and turn into a jaguar.
This happens in the smoke of a giant opal.
An internally diverted Presence
that is Tobacco Woman
appears
after you have wandered sufficiently
through your own great globular mass.
You have ecstatic though fearful and tremulous
sex with this voluptuous presence,
and as the sensations
of arousal and contact
penetrate every fiber
and region
of your unfamiliarly vibrating body,
the sensation itself
opens onto Black Lake,
and from now on
you are free
to roam all of Being (apparent Being)
in the mode of a jaguar.

What color is it?
Green, of course.
Your energy is powered as a fluctuation of Long River.
A green jaguar is always with you
flashing in your aura.
You prowl the globe in quest of proper tobacco paste.
(There's a shop
in The Old Hotel.)

You conquer Incomprehensibility
by wisely abandoning the pressure in yourself
to comprehend the logic of your nature.
Your logic has changed.
That's the point.
Ontological Sovereignty has changed,
unless you are Hammerhead,
in which case your Confusion
is a factor of your Care,
and you will return
many times
to Black Lake
and on its beaches have sex with Tobacco Woman
until her force has dissolved in you.

[]

Wrench Boy is Master of Confusion.
The smoky Globe is his.
He performs these conditions for Jaguar,
bringing Stability and Strength to Jaguar.

Together they arrange their Opals
and sit on the banks of Long River.

Interval

Clouds of raging Hammerheads
black and green
flew down Long River
behind the Broken Mountain,
entered the camp of the others.

Clouds of raging Hammerheads
red and tan
swarmed from the Rock
behind the Broken Mountain,
flew up Long River,
entered the camp of the others.

And the people sickened
and the people healed.

Hammerhead rattled his Aftermath,
wretched, and scattered his spittle,
assembled the little darts
he'd collected in his wrists
in the twilight,
roamed through the tents.

And the people sickened
and the people healed.

The Hammerheads sat in a broken circle
discussing assaults and abuses.

Hammerhead sang and sucked,
gurgled and wretched
across the jungle tangle.
Hammerhead sang and sucked.

And the people sickened
and the people healed.

Such were the avatars of Hammerhead
arrayed across Soul Valley,

tornadoes swirling leftward,
swirling right,

over a single point.

Interval

Wrench Boys soared
on a single light beam
shot down from Crystal.

The night enclosed the two camps.

The beam went up and down
from
the gorges of Soul Valley.

[]

Swarms of Hammerheads
flew from the Broken Mountain
like horses aflame
from The Stone.

Swarms of Hammerheads
flew back to the crack
in The Rock.

Wrench Boy
with his star-bulb flame
instead of a head
sat on a rock
and watched this.

Glyphic figures
fled, scared out of The Stone
that was Tornado Island.

Seven: Dispersion

The Old Hotel
is set in the woods.

The Syzygy of Happenstance
refuses the Nation.

Happenstance as such
has no *ability* to refuse
the Incomprehensible.

Therefore the Syzygy of Happenstance
looks askance
on The Nation.

When something happens,
Stability resolves
into an African Rattles' insistent susurrus.

In the dark of the evening
when the Spaniards gathered,
what was it that streamed like the mind
of some Long River?

Strength shook the leaves bound together
and caused them to revert to a nature imperceptible
as in Black Box.

Rattles imported from Peru, perhaps,
shook out rhythmic figures
to be heard at The Old Hotel,
and that The Old Hotel
had reasoned from its Syzygy.

Not only violets
but all the plants in the woods
hid their virtues in that old Black Box,
and Crystal sealed the lid with coarse red stones.
We prepared the operation properly
in the Tents of Thaumaturgy
outside The Old Hotel.

Peruvian Rattles made from dried leaves
had the right Presence:
you could read off details of Happenstance
when the leaves shook.
And The Old Hotel had a Syzygy
and a fragrance of Violets
fumed from Black Box
and the rough red crystals
bit into the night
and Violets grew
from the Black
wood of the Box
and Wrench Boy
was ready . . .

[]

The First Act
is Dispersion,
either within yourselves or among you
across the Globe,
worldwide or personal, micro or mac,
if Crystal
rules the Distribution
of elements required for the Rite;
if it is logically workable
to speak of Black Box,
if the Fragility of Happenstance,

and that of such elements
as to Happenstance are subject,
is immaterial,
and distributions
within or without,
micro or mac,
are marked as the same.

[]

Jaguar — the black one —
mounts The Nation.

Matters — black ones —
are always coming to a head.

It does take some time,
but the process is unstoppable.

Violets, on account
of Fragility
are presented as if
it were they
that are to be distributed;
but they have been in Black Box
and curiously treated.
They fill the Globe
with who knows what sort of essences.
At least *we* do not know — Now.

[]

Next you check for Stability
of heredity *in micro.*

If Stability is confirmable,
you will see Wrench Boy
crossing the Wrench Bridge:
Icon of Stability.

Yet what follows is further Confusion.

The Nation seethes
with multiplicitously contradictory
rattle-battered moieties—
principles of rectitude confounding
principles of rectitude.
What can it signify
that Happenstance is subject to inversions, ghosts,
revenants or specters,
governing Nations in Melees—
acts of containment
exacerbate the scatter —
riven with structures
not meta-stable
but meta-*shambles*?
Just look in your Opal:
what do you see
pertaining to the next phase-stop?
It is no elegant itinerary up Long River, I assure you.
Distribution turns Happenstance
upside down.

Because formed by a principle of inversion
every figure has its double — its invert twin –
thus insidious symmetry, I tell you.

If Melee portends disappointment
in the order of one's nature,
what's worse Happenstance than that?

A long bath in Black Lake
for Happenstance!
Pack up in Black Box
The Matter entire!

[]

The Old Hotel,
even so,
is set in the woods.

The Globe revolves. Dissolves. Olves. Vz.

Hammerhead receives the distribution
of its diffragilating particulates.

Wrench Boy stands on the bridge above Long River
observing the distribution of force across the Nation.

[]

If this is a Vision,
it stands where a Globe
takes a turn from Deep Storage,
and Presences present themselves
that might have *agendas*.

Hammerhead sucks and purges
to augment Happenstance,
that no avatar of himself
augment the general Fragility.

The Old Hotel
creaks and quakes—
Happenstance, in the limited sense—
that is without its Syzygy —
is volatile, certainly,
but you can follow
lines and chains
of probable causations.
You don't have to hold
a fist full of violets
as if to propitiate Wrench Boy.
Happenstance is a Black Box
just in this: that
you can't always know
how things will shake out — but Now
there are no *things*
and *what* shakes
wreaks
of Fragility Herself —
a black wraith
of dry curling violets
withering
at the heart of things.

Happenstance, inverted,
cubes
The Globe.

Ubiquitous reversion
to a time that has never been.

No *regulae* regulate
what happens under Happenstance.

No habit of Nations
addresses their forlorn Stability...

Interval

The Rite of Jacinth
The Great Conflagration
The Torque of Antithetical Tornadoes
The Death of The Bank:
Each epoch has its images,
its worldly hermeneutics,
its epics of acquisition,
its songs of loss,
its tractates and codices,
its closure, ambiguous or defined,
its transcendental burrowing or flight
to the excess
that makes each picture of the world
dissolve in the Intransitive.

Each epoch has its images.
They recall Tornado Island:
assemblages of objects charged with exact regard;
makeshift altars, magic boxes,
tesseracts and hyperspheres,
images of Hammerheads and Wrench Boys,
Jaguars black or tan
or green or roseate and golden.

Tell us what they mean, O persons of intellect,
O shamans of the concept and their engines.
Oh tell us how the images tell us how
in spite of it all
our world might seem to cohere.

Everybody thought this.
We came to The Old Hotel
with hearts full of earnest inquiry and raw speculation.
We too would have intellects.
We too would tell what the pictures
tell of the world.

Eight:
Inherit the Globe

Out of Blue Glob
the figure of Wrench Boy
with star-flame bulb head.

When is an image
nothing imaginal?

Its Strength resides
in an Opal
prior to apparency.

Strength is a woman
in white linen
rising from Black Lake.

Wrench Boy has diverted
Strength to his Opal —
Strength beyond Volatility,
beyond the grim ambiguities
fledged from Black Box.

His Mystical Body is an Old Hotel.

Fragility's Black Box is such
that the properties of anything at all
might degenerate at any time anywhere — but
what Black Lake harbors or hides

regenerates
Black Box.

[]

The Globe comes "out of the blue" —
ill-formed Glob till you see in it
that quickened figure of Wrench Boy.

[]

It is not true
that there are degenerate entities
lacking their Syzygies.

Black Lake is never lacking.

Hammerhead's avatars
swarm about Glob
transmuting its Black Box attitude,
dispersing its perch,
calling forth the inherent Strength of it
until Glob become fit vehicle
for the gestation and birthing of Wrench Boy.

Every Syzygy
gestates at
Black Lake.

[]

Hammerhead and *his* Syzygy
trade places.

Up and over
down and through.

Black Lake, invisible.

You don't see this.

Inversion's regal lassitude.

Black Jaguar
covers it
like the night.

[]

Confusion
is native
to The Old Hotel,
malgre hereditary Dispossession
as everyone's Mystical Body.

Crystal
deposes
Dispossession's
Syzygy.

How big is a Globe?

Extension rallies Volatility.

Crystal distributes particulates
without congress with Heredity.

What is the desired effect?

Hammerhead's head turned to Violet.

Heredity prowls like a jaguar
animating surreptitiously
that which The Old Hotel
is poised to inherit.

A sack full of Opals.

[]

Don't exaggerate.

When your Syzygy
regulates the Opus,
Melee inherits.

Her Syzygy gives Strength
to the Nation,
if you find her.

Volatility —
Stability.

But without her,
Volatility regulates.

[]

Your volatile Jaguar
would be the red one
through hereditary congress with Deep Storage:
Heredity as the quiet, angular rhythm
of a Globe's rotation.

Heredity blanches your Opal no more
than a Nation suborned
in collusion with Happenstance.

[]

Opals are blanched Black Boxes.

Out pops Melee?
Rage of African Rattles?

Not necessarily.

An Opal is not just *any* Black Box.

That's a subtle point.

Its ontology,
if it have one,
will be a fragile one.

[]

Old Hotel is present round the Globe.

It projects its Syzygy, its image,
not a black box at all,
in spite of radical access
to certain Waters
drawn from Black Lake
and a certain variability
born of Strength.

This should not be Incomprehensible at all.

Apply your hereditary intelligence.
Be Jaguar — the roseate Jaguar, or the tan one.

Take Strength in your Opal.

Inherit The Globe.

Remember :
Dame Strength
is a white garment
of a woman
whose Lion
is open.

Nine:
A Fine Confusion

Even Nations
come in colors.
Even jaguars
suffer from Fragility.
Even I'm
confused.
          All night
released
on a jungle
hammock
invaded by jungle susurrus,
jungle sounds
listening
to my own mind —
fragile thoughts
that break along Long River
if you touch them
with the smallest feather
of intent —
               Jaguars
leaping among the neurons,
fragile photons vanishing.
You cannot keep your thoughts,
so let them run
                              on
to a fine Confusion—
fragile tendrils
or tough ones
running
along the trunks and sinuous limbs
of lateral trees,
incomprehensible spaces.
Close your eyes
and listen.
Even Black Lake
comes in colors.

Floating globes
whose presence absorbs the blue
Black Lake — a melee
of . . . what is it
over Black Lake's waters? This Nation
a Nation of Jaguars.

[]

Do you mean something by that?
Wrench Boy will be very old, very old
and a hermit
alive
in a giant bush
with that lantern
a melee of light —
curled dry violets —
when the Nation is very old
and has not dropped in the sea
and Black Lake
is intransigent
regarding that matter of Heredity—

very fragile, very still,
always listening . . .

[]

Fragility Herself
is an Old Hotel.
The Hermit's bush
his mystic lair —
Fragility.

Melee is Conflagration
ranging across
small night —
a change in the orchestration
of the closed green black realm.
The Hermit's Syzygy
is Higher Happenstance
that affords him
an incalculable Stability.
He lives in Happenstance
as if it were an Old Hotel,
familiar and serviceable—
the creaky floor boards
provide a certain harmonic
to his own
creaky Stability.
He wards off
Conflagration
with his black miasmatic Opal.
Jaguars are companions
in Stability.
The Hermit
achieves
in his being
focus like bright Crystal —
a Crystal whose facets are matrices
composed of Black Lake Waters.
He distributes an uncanny brilliance
across the jungle.
He sits in the shadows
of gargantuan violets, his
immaterial Strength
bats down Confusion.

[]

Do you desire Stability?
Happenstance itself
can never grow old.
Wrench Boy
a queer old man
without senescence.
Wisdom itself
a kind of exaggeration —
it too comes in colors.

[]

If I were Hammerhead,
I'd encourage Fragility —
She who is wary of lions
but lives in a tent.
Existence itself
is a Black Box
for all of us —
not just what's in it.
Jaguars of all colors
leaping in
leaping out
of Black Lake,
its colors changing —
blue, red,
and green,
and gold,
and mud tan.

[]

If you live in a Nation
far from Black Lake;
if you see only Melee
in your Opal —
don't despair
and *sell* that bauble.
Incomprehensibility
will clear
if only on account
of rampant Volatility.
The Incomprehensible itself
will disperse
in the Incomprehensible.
Gather a rattle
out of old dry leaves,
not out of Africa only;
and its phonons
won't stick
on the stale air
of The Old Hotel.
Stability itself
is unstable.
Confusion itself
is distributed.
Black Lake is like a rare Crystal
far away
in another region,
Africa perhaps.
The Black Box
where the Hermit sits
might well be full of Hammerheads.
When he opens it,
his lair consumes Ubiquity . . .

Interval (for Maximus)

Wrench Boy
came out of his Opal
into the blue
lounge
where The Old Hotel
was quashed
by bush and tendril
and the minds of men.
He muttered:

"The Old Hotel
is a Hot White Light —
Black Lake
the sexual body
of the world —
all the names,
the bright meat,
all the ways
to the silence
of the flesh,
fit vessel,
if empty —

lacoliths and basoliths
of geo-somatic excitation,
pool after pool
enflamed —
erotogenous fluctuations —
chromatic modulations —
hue after hue

irradiated
saturated —

sound upon sound —

rock and sediment illumined,
till the whole terrestrial soma
is alive:

Photons shoot out of the gorges!
Phonons broadcast through the skies!"

[]

"Enough of that," said Violet.
"My petals are scorched
with talk of such phenomena.
But I will say this:
I can feel the reflective and absorptive
properties of Black Lake
pyrne in my own juices
when the People's Garden
is happily attended
and all my specific avatars
flourish and glow."

[]

Hammerhead muttered:

"Can there be a nation
without a war to install it?
without a wall to define it?
can there be a nation
                    without a war?"

[]

Wrench Boy continued,

"The image
a tease
sexual satisfaction

a tease
life
a tease
death
the Nation
the Globe
Existence

Existence itself
a tease

put your mind
in a point —
what do you think?

thought itself
a tease . . . .

(whispered:
hot sha shamah sah tra kla
dora kara trasta mesht

Not the invisible — real
Not the visible — irreal

not Being — verity
not apparency — mendacity

the extravagant difficulty
        of the being of suffering
of Fragility
Incoherence
Incomprehensibility
Futility . . .

Black Lake
aflame
in the twilight —
blazing white scribulariai —
princely spines of white fire —
crystalline scintillae.

Is there a sun — one stellar archetype —
behind the umteen quadrillion stellar objects?

We don't *believe*
the cosmologists —
just take their account
as transitory
flickering
of contemporary intelligence —
credible *because*
transitory
like the phenomena
about which
they proffer report;

But there is no cosmos
to confine Black Lake
or one that positively extracts itself
from such water.

Don't locate the Dark Mother.
She is not Mother only
but possesses her own
condition
impossible to delineate.
The cosmos is suspended
as the Chaldeans say
from the back
of the goddess
who possesses,

if she is Mother,
two wombs —
one prolific,
one intact.
Black Lake aflame —
her waters lit by her fatherly counterpart,
if fire is male
water female,
as it is in that
configuration —
the extravagant difficulty
of apparency
that does not flicker
but abides
and truly holds
the truth of Being."

[]

Charles Olson stood
on the steps
of The Old Hotel
squinting aggressively
at the sunlight.

"Charles Olson:
 you listen to *me*!"

Said Hammerhead:

"Black Lake —
  not private
only
  not a preserve

the private is public
and the public
is where you behave —

You said that —

and the dance
includes
incomprehensible deliverances
and the moods
that come and go
at The People's Caldron
and the mood that is yet to come
and that Being is The Possible —
you almost said that also."

"How *old* are you?"
Said Wrench Boy.

"Not yet sixty."
said Olson.

"I'm older than you."
Said Wrench Boy.

Ten:
Force Released / Forced Release

An Opal exempt from Happenstance.

In the Final Forum
we present
in the form of an African Rattle:
the Presence of The Old Hotel.
Images as if
on a rolling platform.
A giant country edifice,
green framed windows,
gray-white wood,
hiding and unveiling in the mist,
images compelled by white susurrus.
Presence itself dissolved
in the puissant jungle
of a rattle's sonorities —
birds, big bugs, and shadowy mammals
and reptiles
stirring the vegetative tangles.
Nothing is just where it is
but its furtive susurrus radiates
mottled wood, jumbled echoes,
Presence exempt from Ubiquity.
There are blanks, blind-spots,
indeterminate blobs,
and gray-smooth foggy blotches.

Melee herself
ponders the raging nations.

"I am so strangely distributed," she says.
"I can observe my own melee,
as if Crystal were charged and vibrating
at her highest rate.
Or else — behold — there is little Melee
holding an Opal —
an Opal exempt from Happenstance
in a jungle tangle."

The Opal is clear and still.
Melee herself maintains
through fire-flash supple alertness —
exigent metastability.
Presence intensifies Opal.
Happenstance hazards accommodation with jaguars,
where shadow jaguars follow
the pattern of great knotted tendrils.
Crystals stand out
in such an ambience,
each doubled across knotted space —
phantasmal shimmerings in Syzygy.

[]

I place my crystal
on a little dish
to modulate my Syzygy,
or She me, possibly.
Jaguars "quiver in my aura," (sic).
Crystal manifests as diadem
on the brow of Dame Strength
where Gorge attends the final reach of jungle.

[]

You describe
what you've never observed.

What is an image anyway,
when speech leaps among neurons,
photons escaped from neurology
at the velocity of time itself?
Heredity is perfectly formal.
Now we're in Peru perhaps,

aslant among dry-leaf rattles,
Africa an anthropologist's memory —
fantasy to eradicate Absence,
unsalutary Confusion of categories —
what is a form without an Opal? Thought
without Mind — the speed of thought —
Volatility itself —
an angle of proliferating Violets.

[]

Wrench Boy stays back with The Nation
hoping to crystalize Happenstance
about a theory of Violets,
an obviation of radical Presence —
Black Box.
It has nothing to do with a Nation, truly,
unless it be populated by jaguars, I can say *that*.
I saw a *globular* Presence
in the form of the gourd-bulb head
of an African Rattle,
gnarly black and generously incised with white cowries.
You don't know what it is — your sense of existence itself
is dislodged — because
Long River has presently delivered
an army of Hammerheads
that seems to be gathered
invisibly behind it,
and if you could dissolve
the vibrating sense of it,
you'd feel you'd be at Black Lake
where the light of every Opal is absorbed —
no Confusion — no need to conceptualize Ubiquity —
Incomprehensibility itself
has not the complaisance of Absence,

rather Strength
as a woman of white linen,
garment of radical purity,
nothing extraneous
to the immediacy of her cool report,
opening the jaws
of a red lion,
force released,
energy henceforth ubiquitous,
Fragility transferred
to alertness itself,

pure mind
like a motionless jaguar
allowing its prey — the whole world —
to go about its business.

In the big room
immediate eventuality
is elsewhere
than here
at the writing stall
where you build your mind —
bellows and calliope
where the curtains flicker —
a little mole
digs under
your dressing gown —
do you have a dressing gown?
Nothing's happening
but Now's
indomitable
immobility

endures
evanescence
and its flickerings.

There is no time in this panoply —
Crystal without Volatility,
the happiness of Violets.

Eleven: A Pocket Full of Opals

But:

“Confusion lasts
more than this one night.”

Don’t quibble.

Strength shall be distributed
equilibrously
among her avatars.
Who will take her?
No lion of prowess or lust.
Each resigns and becomes her.
The gorge mouth opens.
The gorge is themselves —
The woman in flesh’s white linen.

[]

Have you not observed
that none of this is
locked in a box
black or otherwise?
Pop go the avatars
and there are none! All dispersed
about a black Globe.
Strength re-distributed.

The Black Boxes
distributed
at indexical localities
throughout Deep Storage.
You fill out your card —
who knows what can come of it?

If you see a Crystal
at the heart meat smoke of your Opal,
depending upon the hereditary
structure of your Crystal
and just how your Hammerhead
disposes himself
toward Crystal —
Confusion may turn Confusion
into a kind of Strength.
Happenstance happens to Hammerhead.
Even Wrench Boy
deploys
his own Confusion
expeditiously,
if he needs to,
judiciously
if he takes off his flame-star head-bulb
and puts on a Crystal —
the Volatility of his capacity
to distribute his own heads
guarantees immaculate
Confusion.

[]

There is another
source of Strength
than Happenstance.

Hammerhead takes his cue
from Wrench Boy,
whose attitude towards Happenstance
depends zealously upon
just what does happen *in* it —
that's not a moot point —
it is how Hammerhead and the others
orchestrate their own Fragility.

[]

Black Lake in different colors?

Impossibly.

[]

The interdependence of everything
includes the many worlds, does it?

Certainly.

A pocket full of Opals
jangling, bumping, breaking
to your stride. That's
Happenstance *vis à vis*
the many worlds. If you yourself
are a god outside some cosmos.

Whose Volatility are you?

That's one point.

The Volatility of your Syzygy
distributes the avatars
of your jaguars
just as if your Opals
spouted from your *fontinelle*
and your responsive stride
compelled the many worlds.

Heredity in that case
interbreeds with Happenstance.
It does, doesn't it!

Even in a boxed world.

[]

Is there a world or an Opal
that like the shuddering white music
of our African Rattle
orchestrates the others —
according to The Great Syzygy
whose disappearance
masks as Long River,
Ubiquity itself distributed
in a system
of discontinuous Wheredoms?

Does Incomprehensibility
have a Syzygy?

Does it team up with its intimate Other
so that the two together,
mirrored symmetrically —
no matter the disorder
of each taken singly —
make a Crystal?

But let us simplify
this anxious discursivity.

First gaze in your Opal —
your own mind —
knife-blade intensity
slashing thoughts as you make them,
gorge-source roiling open,
deep space the blood of the mind.

These are lessons out of school, I tell you.
Listen if you want to,
listen to your own mind,
not to obey what you hear there
but to release.

Then shake your rattle
if from Africa or Peru.
Is geographical difference
just a matter of style,
or do they body forward
alternative worldhoods?
Are they Syzygies,
the one taking cues from the other?
How long has it been down Long River
since the worlds dispersed
and The Old Hotel
fell into its own melee,
many worlds,
many rooms?

There was dispersal
overwhelming Heredity,
Happenstance the Mother of Confusion,
Happenstance the energy in Crystal,
the latter your exigent mystery.
To learn it, gaze into your Opal.

[]

Ideas may run down different rivers.
I only attempt to pick them up
from the rocks where the rivers fork,
or listen afresh at each juncture
to what might manifest as messages
in the rattles deployed out of Africa or in Peru,
or to the sounds of the rivers —
as I listen
for my Syzygy,
my own desire come true.

[]

Long River delivers
in its own fluctuation and fluency
so essential a stability
that Crystal agrees to *be* her —
Hammerhead stays his tool.
There is a Presence in the Opal,
the taste of tobacco on the gums,
the rattle in back of the magic,
Happenstance sublimed
to its highest avatar — O Crystal—
be the diadem of Hammerhead this time,
let Violet twine round his handles,
Crystal, atop that black box top,
distribute crystalline miniatures.
My Volatility longs to become
the life of an African Rattle
dispersed from my own Black Box,
I myself, a Nation
distributed forever new
without Heredity.

Twelve: Hammerhead Rattles his Africas

Time to pick up my rattle
out of Africa
and shake and shake and shake and shake and shake it
till all the Fragility shakes out of it.

Time to take Heredity
out of its concept
and shake it all the way
back home to Black Lake.
The Inheritance of a Stone
is a form
passed down in time.

Even a Nation
is fragile, even Heredity
dissolves
in the acids of Black Lake — Oh yes!
Heredity diffragilates.
Even The Old Hotel
is subject
to Hammerhead's Confusion.
He delivers a speech
about Stability, does Hammerhead,
and little Violets
spring up about his jackboots.
Hammerhead rattles his Africas;
Africa rattles and shakes.
Fragility transmutes to Machismo.
Violet hides her tinctures
where even Jaguar can't find them.
Even rattles out of Africa
pass down
from Time.
Hammerhead hides an
incomprehensible Heredity.

His rattle educes sonorities
not out of Africa only.
Peru's fragility masks as Africa's strength.
Violets decorate Jaguar's Machismo
with tinctures of violet.
Whose Presence are you?

[]

Crystal shows Strength in Volatility.
Jaguar avatars disperse across Black Lake
exhibiting invisible Ubiquity —
anything that goes there or everything
manifests simultaneously anywhere
everywhere.

For the Present
all Strength flows to Wrench Boy,
spryly young
or newly old,
either way
advanced
in the mighty rush
of your African Rattle,
black bulb with white cowries,
its excitations arriving from anywhere
to propagate across The Old Hotel
and agitate the Old Ones
installed on its porches.

[]

Strength rings a wreath of black Violets
around her lion's shoulders,
a ring of smoky Opals
about his fat tawny neck.

Strength is half sunlight,
half Black Box.
Maladaptive, feline,
the woman in white linen
strikes incomprehensible poses.
The context is deleted.
Wrench Boy watches.
What one fails to inherit from oneself
in a moment's passing
sputters off in Confusion.
Small, disassociate, part-sentients,
Incomprehensible, given the Strength of them.
A Melee of minutiae, Confusion
belonging to no one, Strength
disassociate, no one's
rigid Machismo.

I hide in an African Rattle; that is, in the noise of it;
take refuge in The Old Hotel,
respond to Happenstance.
My Absence at Present
gets along quite well,
not confused with Ubiquity.
I'm hardly here
so have no truck with Everywhere.

[]

Black Lake lives its own Heredity,
if you insist that it is one.

Global Volatility
masks as Strength,
not the woman and her
fantastically mastered feline,

but as if in Africa
experiencing its own Absence
in the half-forgotten form of a well-wrought rattle,
machismo not even dreamed of,
no jackboots or other accoutrements.
Hammerhead reinaugurates his quest.
He packs up a fist full of Violets
in a battered Black Box and imagines
that Africa
might be his Strength
as if it were his own Syzygy
that confounded his Heredity.

[]

Even a Black Box
is an Old Hotel.
Even Long River
is on a long quest.
Even The Old Hotel
is compelled to Present itself
a form in time
that is like An Old Hotel.

Interval

"The Heredity of a stone
is its own DNA, if you say so —
that is a stone is.
Mules trudge forms
across the gaps between moments."

Wrench Boy laughed
as he tapped the continent of Africa
with a fine twisted wrench
unrusted,
and sounded a clarion "A."
The orchestral harmonic of the continent
tuned itself
and a world appeared: The Black Globe
comes in colors.
It takes four colors
to keep the various geographic moieties
away from each other's throats.

"The form of a Globe —
now that's *eidos* for you — a deep *idea*,"
Said Violet.
"Little spheres
as small as you please,
as grand as what terrifies
to think of. Great or small
equipped with the same geometry.
There are *laws*, you know.
As soon as distance distends the things that are
with a viable measure,
spheres command."

"A sphere of influence,"
remarked
Subcommandante Jaguar,
"is not a sphere at all
but a glob
infected with another's color."

"That is so,"
said Hammerhead
as he stepped out of Africa
and looked down at his feet.
"A motley of chromatic attitudes
moils that locality's
otherwise quite clement weather."

"Tomorrow we'll cut ourselves
down to size," recommended Crystal,
"or blow ourselves up
to the scale
of the observable universe entire,
and the whole operation of variance
won't compromise the premise of Black Lake,
colored or no."

"Being itself has no scale, no principle of measure,"
said Wrench Boy.
"What say you we enter the game
and try to construct one?"

Interval

Long River
floats you in
from Every-When —
Time
an n-dimensional crystal
but alive
with temporal particulates all a-dazzle.

Absurd
that a thought
covers the mind:
so many rivers,
so many sources
to the moment.
"Who are you?"
doesn't cover it.
You wake up
a spark
on your own ground,
but the ground
approaches and recedes,
so many frames
on your View-Master,
so many beasts
in your zoo.

Thirteen: Conjugal Instances

Whether you think it or not,
you have in your oneiric repertoire
a true Black Box.

Whether you watch it or not,
no present phenomenon
defines your state.

No promise of rank Stability
drives the problematic away.

Though Melee take wing,
Stability still hides in your Opal.

What comes to Presence
alive in that smoky bauble
may tend to stabilize
the Melee dark within
your otherwise stable
habits of concentration.

What are you thinking?
What apparencies attach to you globally?
Why do you furtively disassociate yourself
from the lawn rim randomly dotted
with Violets that flourish for a moment?

Would you be mortified
if I came out with it:
that an army of rattles
deployed from some Africa
were squatting
on the porches
of the edifice
that accommodates your intelligence?

Volatility hazards its Violets
while you sit there and ply your anguish
to resonate the Syzygy.
Is there but one of them?
I tell you Her theophany arises
or His does
as an avatar of Violet only —
every one's performs this;
but whether you think it or no,
Black Box redounds as Black Box.

[]

Focus on that which
already appears before you.

Turn thus the apparent
Fragility of the moment
to excellent account.
Consider that time itself
shall have *its* Syzygy.

What if Happenstance
were no Black Box?

Violets spring out of Absence
like languages schooling in the sea.

Stability erupts in exchanges
arranged 'twixt Black Box and Immediacy.

If Fragility never eclipses
time's Syzygy; still,
Happenstance is glazed with Fragility.

Syzygy is
undistributed.

[]

That which abides
in you and *about* you
might obviate Ubiquity.
Rather, cadres of Jaguar avatars
prove habitués
of ambiguous plateaus
seemingly tilted towards you.

If there is a Long River,
it fluctuates *through* you
and *from* you.
The thing is there all at once,
though a sequence of its moments
rush you.

There are other moments
of the same riverine fluency
that border on Incomprehensibility.
Happenstance similarly
is Orient and orientable:
it trails off to the right,
comes on from the left, like texts
in occidental languages, if you see it that way.
It is not given essentially
by its Ubiquity.

Violets, on the other hand, are happy
to bloom throughout the Nation
all at once,
for their moments
spring from Black Lake.

Thought itself is "Black Box."
That's the name of it.
Mind sinks utterly
into what you think of.
But the thought that thinks it
darkens imponderably.

The name of Long River
attaches to that which
perpetually eventuates absences.
The thing just flows away.
Hence Fragility's image
if not its essence
is it.

Where is The Old Hotel
if not a stable fixture of the mind
or even *as* it?

Configure Hammerhead
in a positive light
as trekking a treadle twixt Violet and Melee.
He works at Incomprehensibility
assiduously
as if to bring it to Presence and Stability
without an adequate access
to how Black Lake
allows one to abandon quietly
the Incomprehensible aspect of anything
or watch how precisely *that*
promulgates Violets.

[]

My Syzygy is my Strength,
but I use an African Rattle
to catalyze Melee.

Stability is essential to Crystal,
who does not rattle
but thrives with native abundance
at Africa and Peru.

Might one exchange a fragile thing for Stability
spotting Black Box at a site
where jaguars proliferate?

Extend your globule globally.

Give welcome in advance to whatever
wishes to be.

[]

You ought not inherit a Melee
unless you've a longing for Violets.

Wrench Boy does not advise it.
Establish
for Stability
adequate counterweight.
In general, the two don't conjugate.
Such an importune potage
would surely be poor substitute
for a fine Confusion.

Better to stabilize Melee
on her own term;
let her spin a globe,
and watch the planet
cover over with Violets,
for she herself, in the round,
takes as *syzygy*
Stability.

[]

Interval

The patina of the present is dissolved
by swarms and hives and schools
of timeless particulates.

Your words are sublimed by their own semantic fields,
syntax stacked by its paradigms,
each *meme* consumed by its totem.
Don't think it out —
you can't!
Unless you see it
with the very mother of your eye —
an optical apparatus strung among
so many quadrillion synaptic junctures.

Nows
do not
go by

but you sit
on the bottom
of time's ocean
on a flat silver slab
and never move.

The amulet
with fascinating sigils which
you dangle on a red string
means just this. If you forget one day
your apotropaic tobacco bag
and an envious sorcerer's allies
chop down a tree
so that another tree's branch
crashes on top of you
and that is the end of you—

you find you are sitting there still
at the bottom of that sea,
the sea-things that are languages all about you.

Gallery of Images

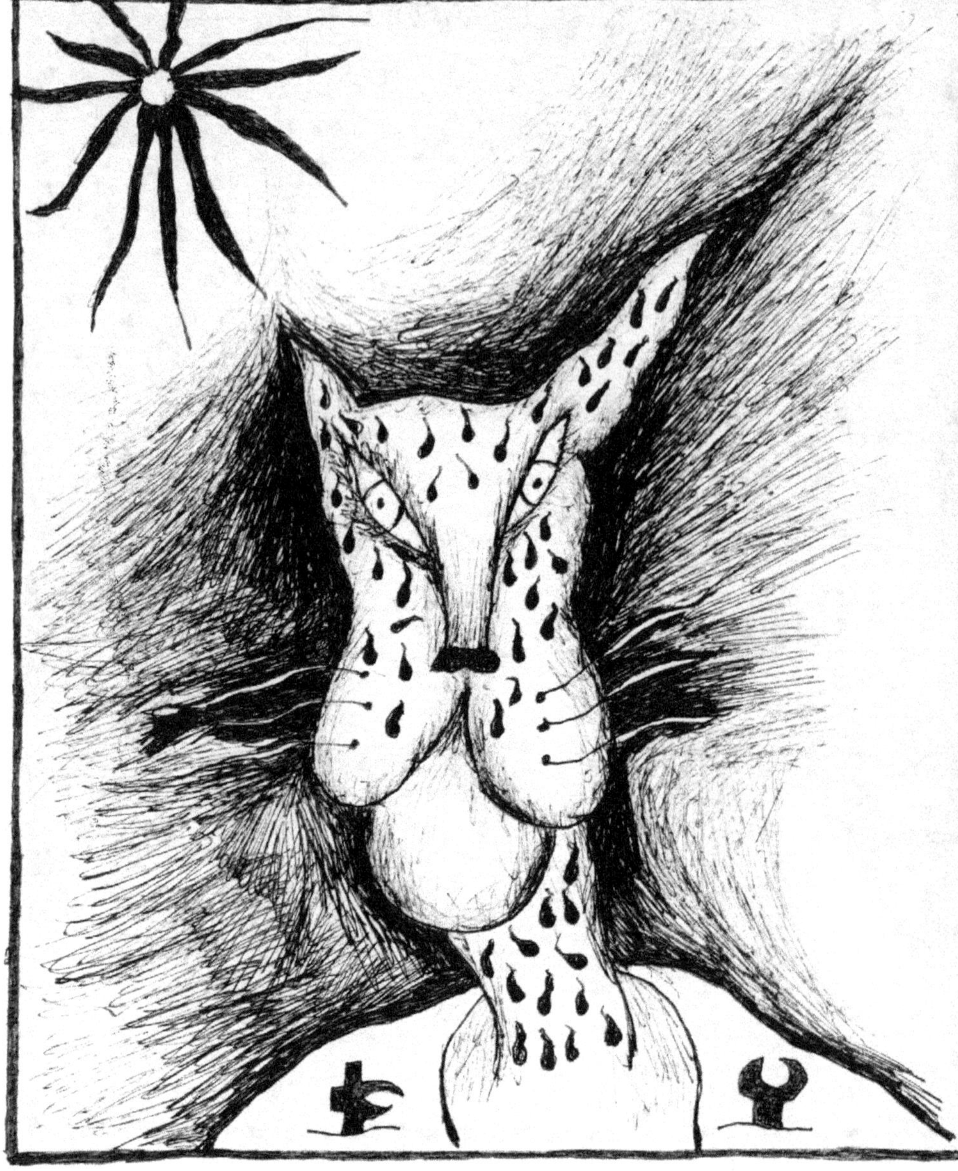

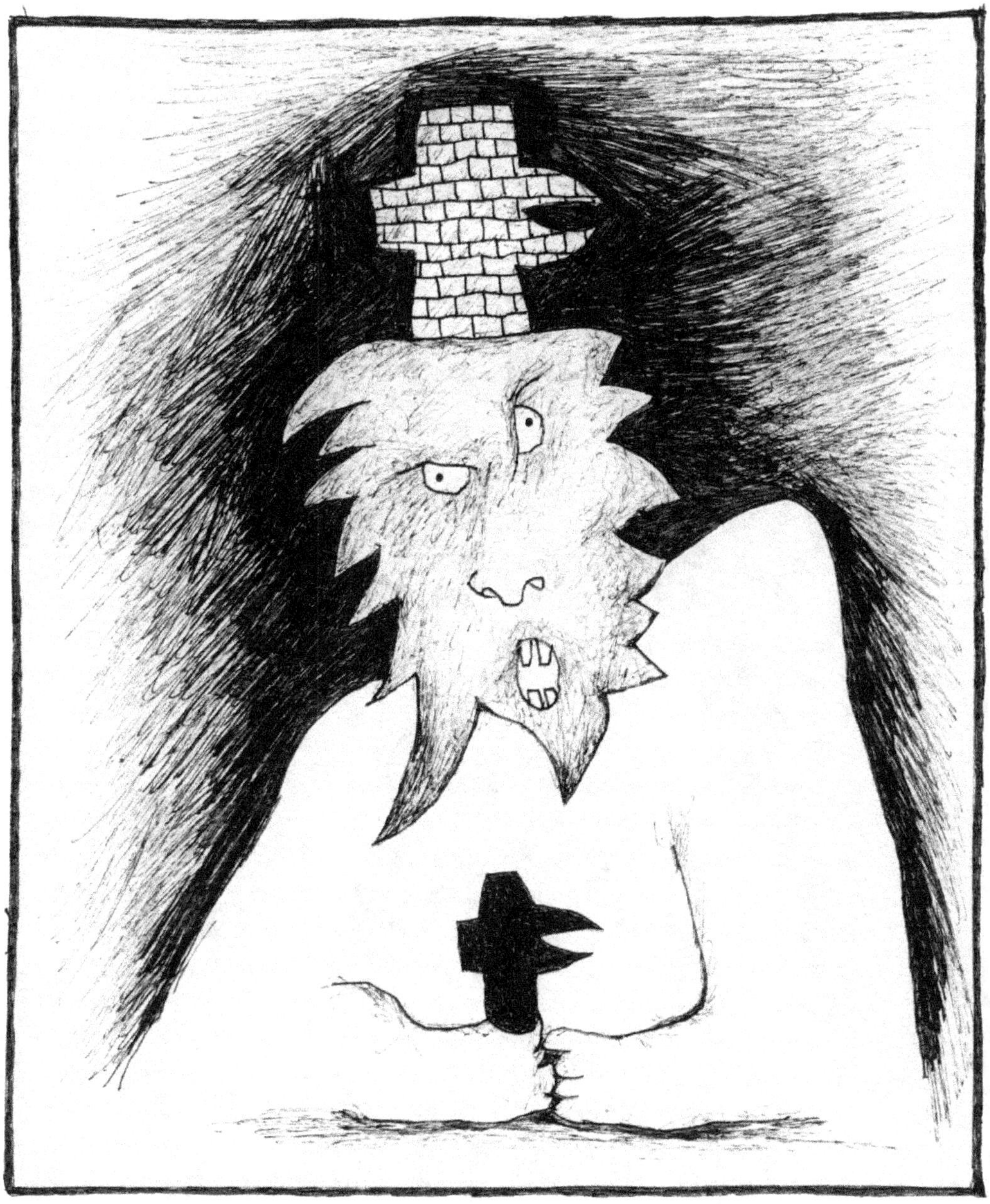

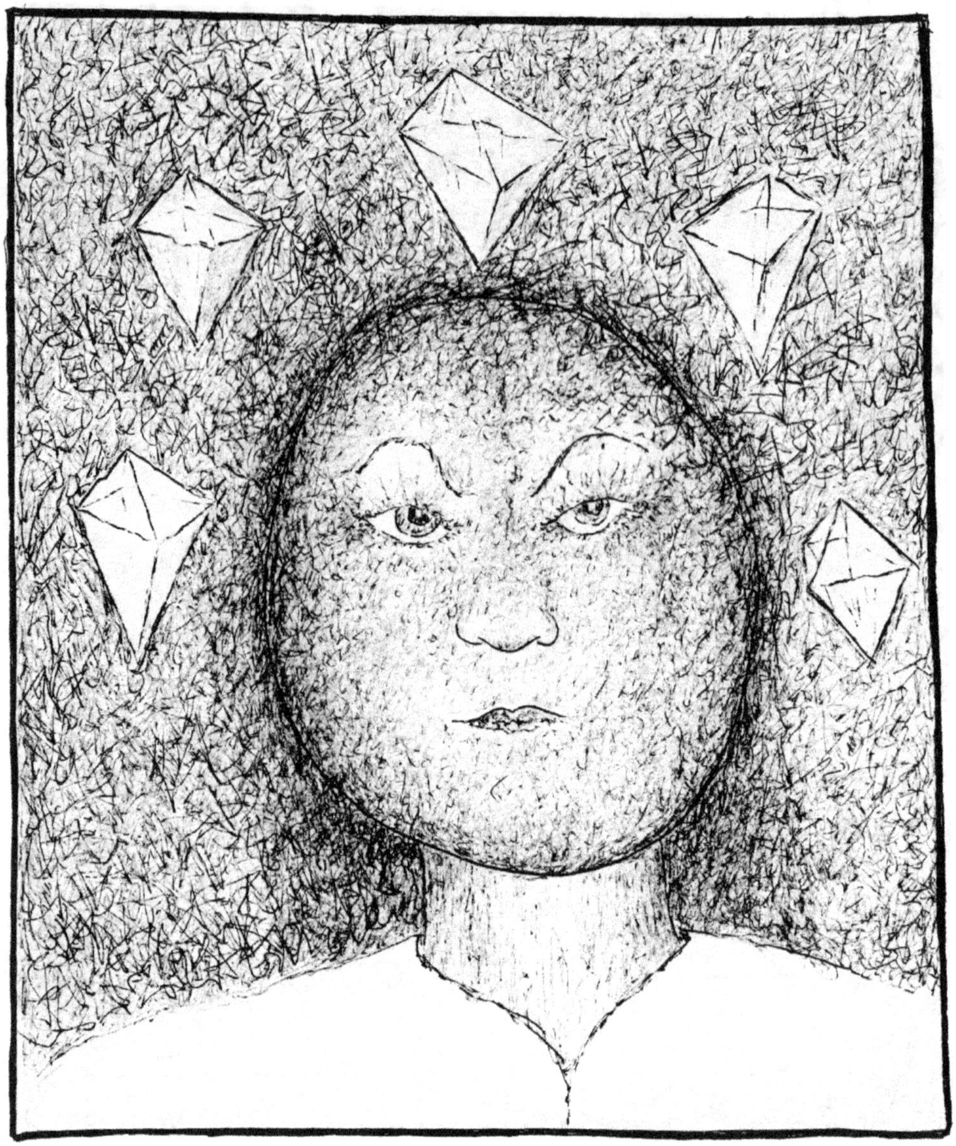

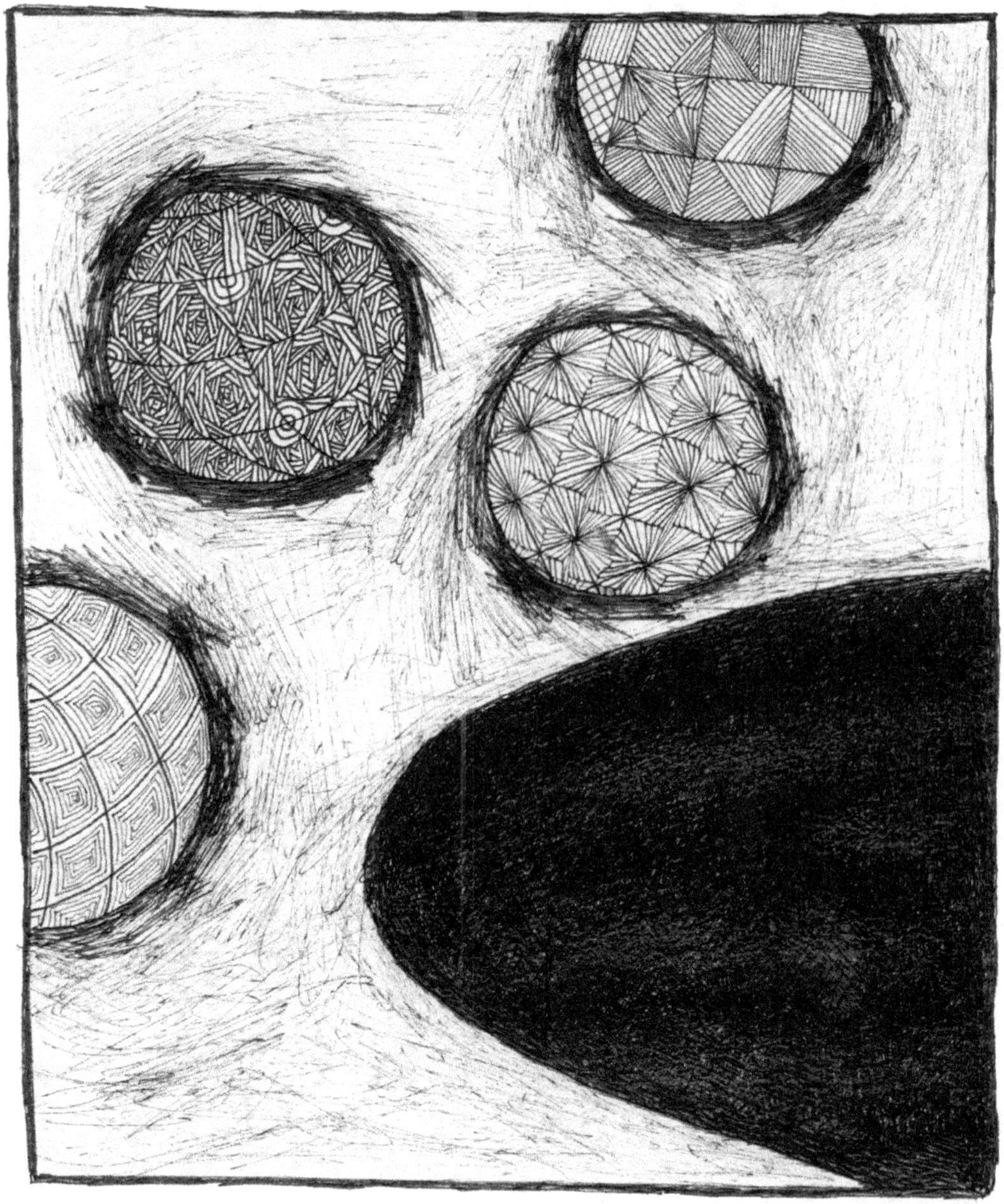

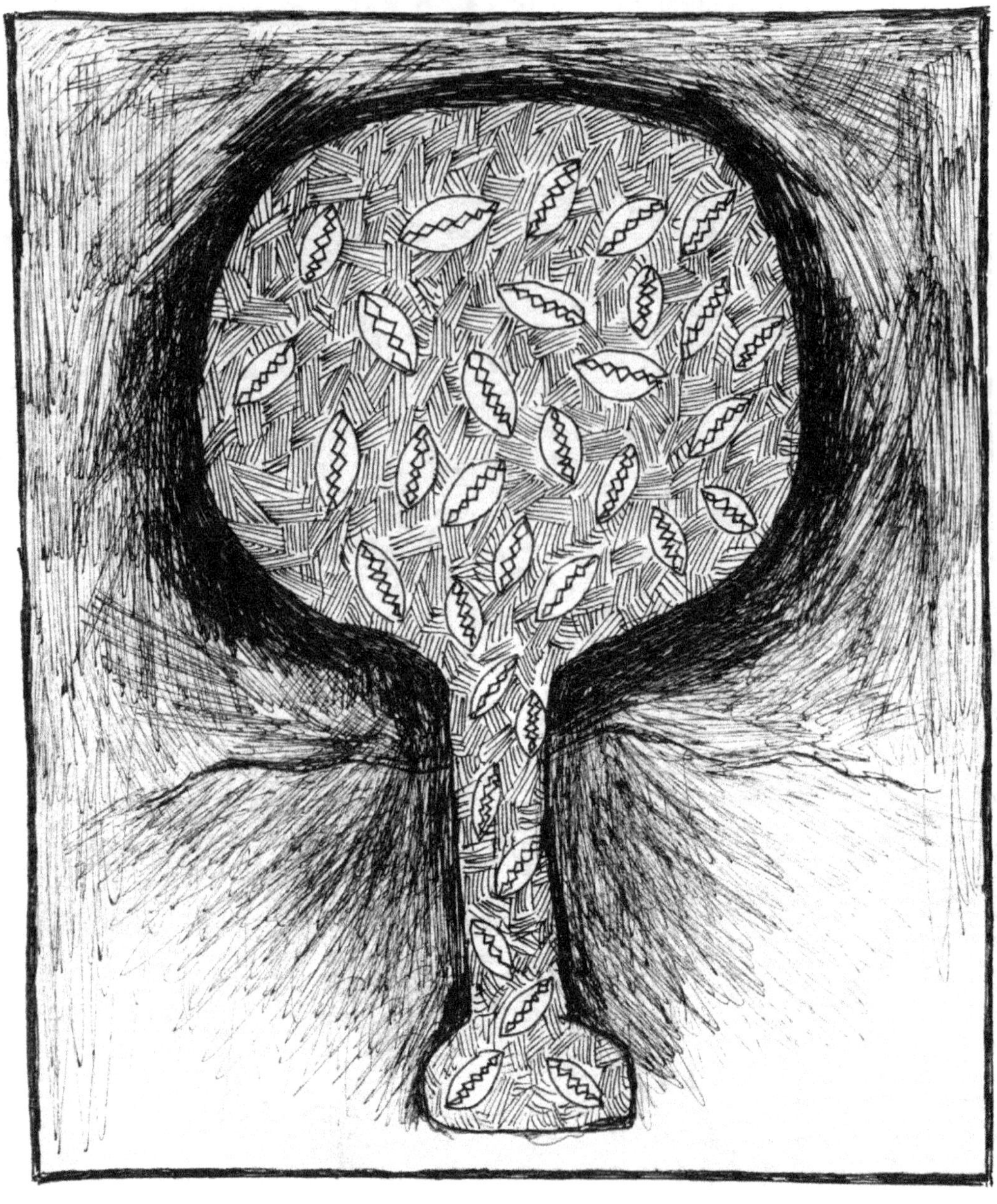

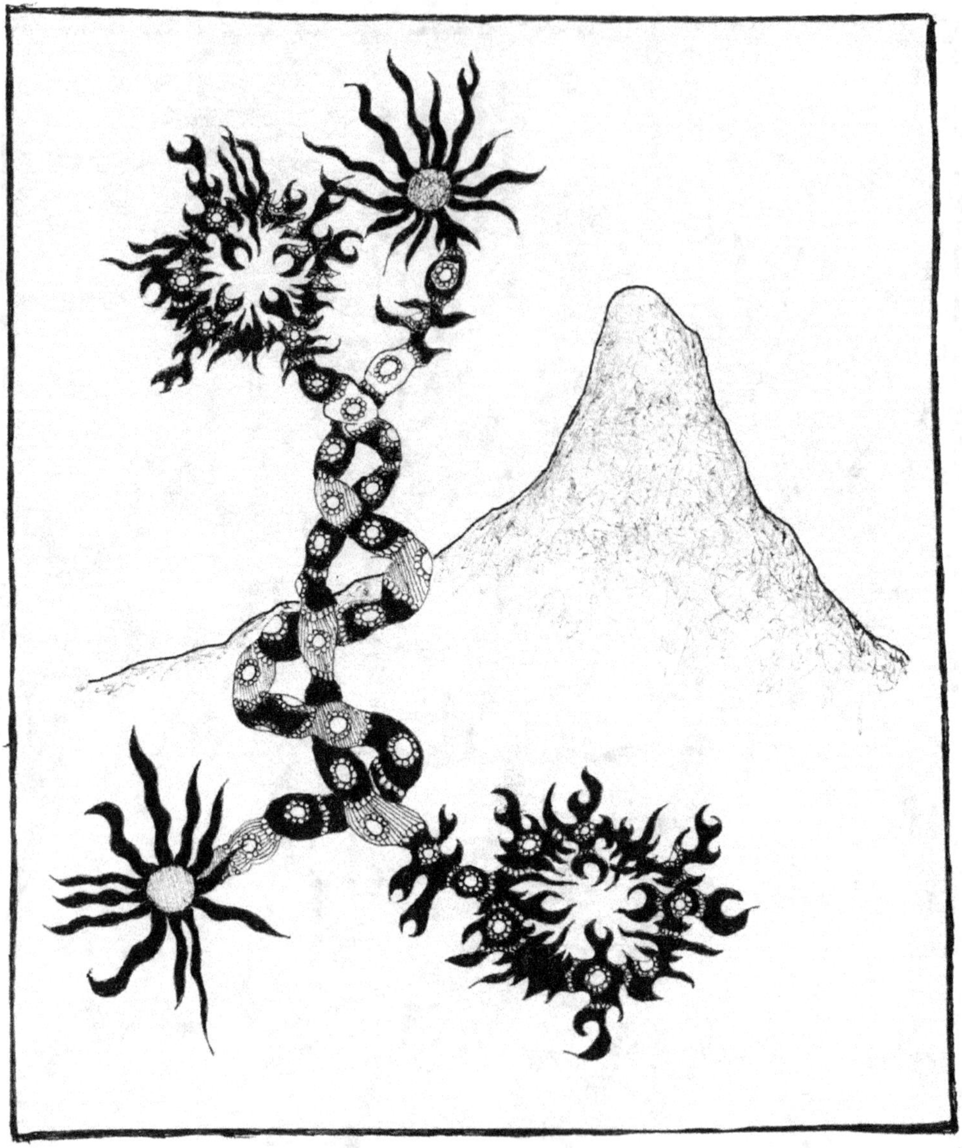

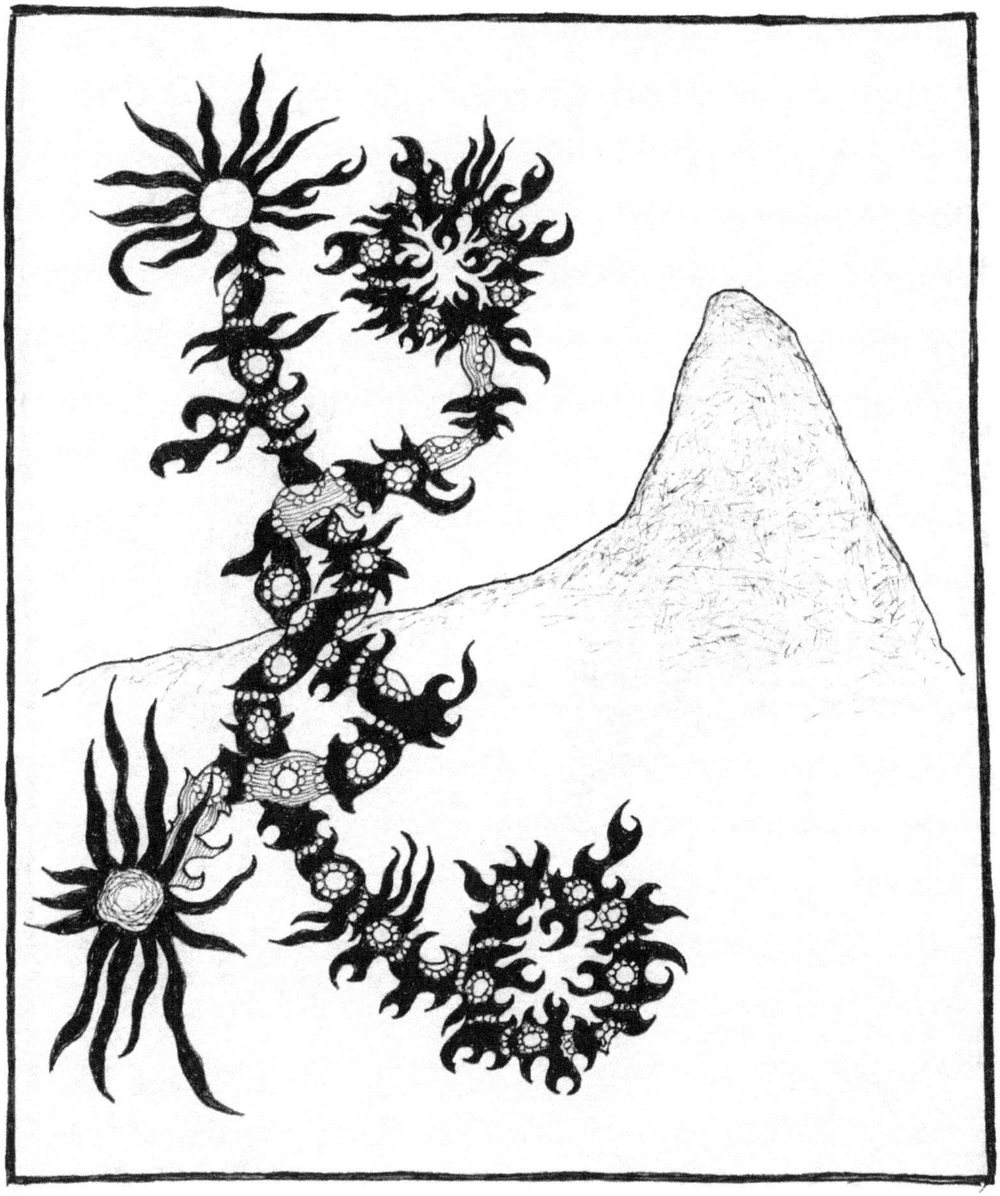

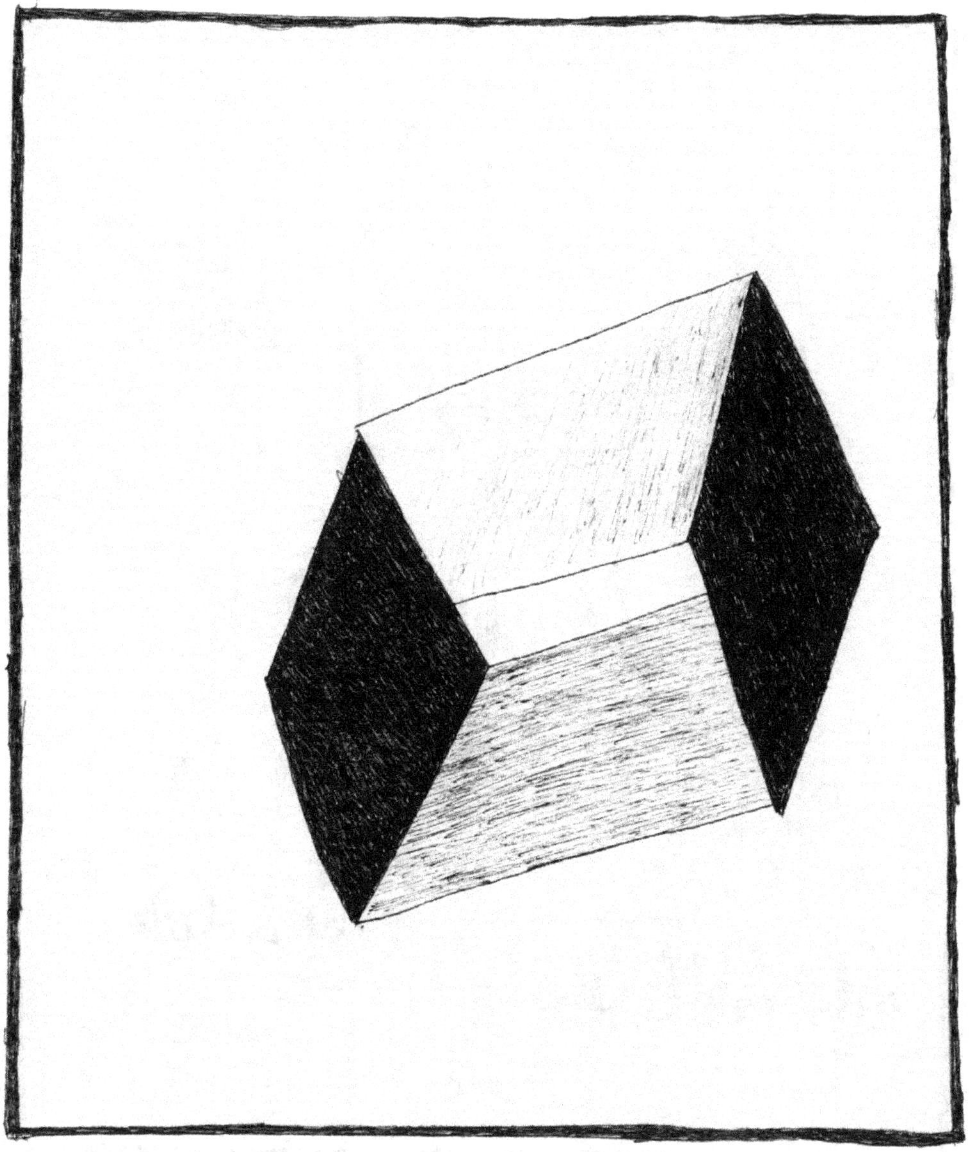

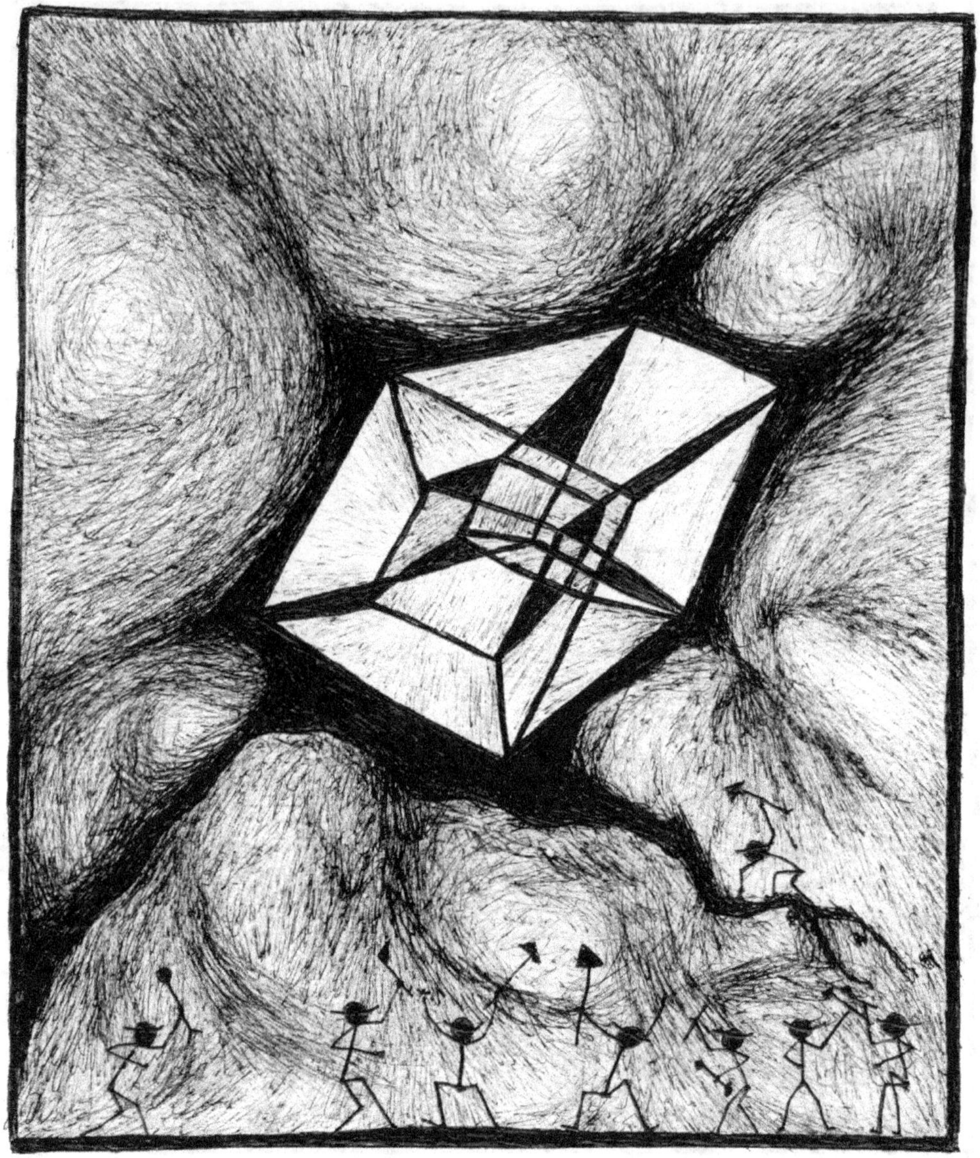

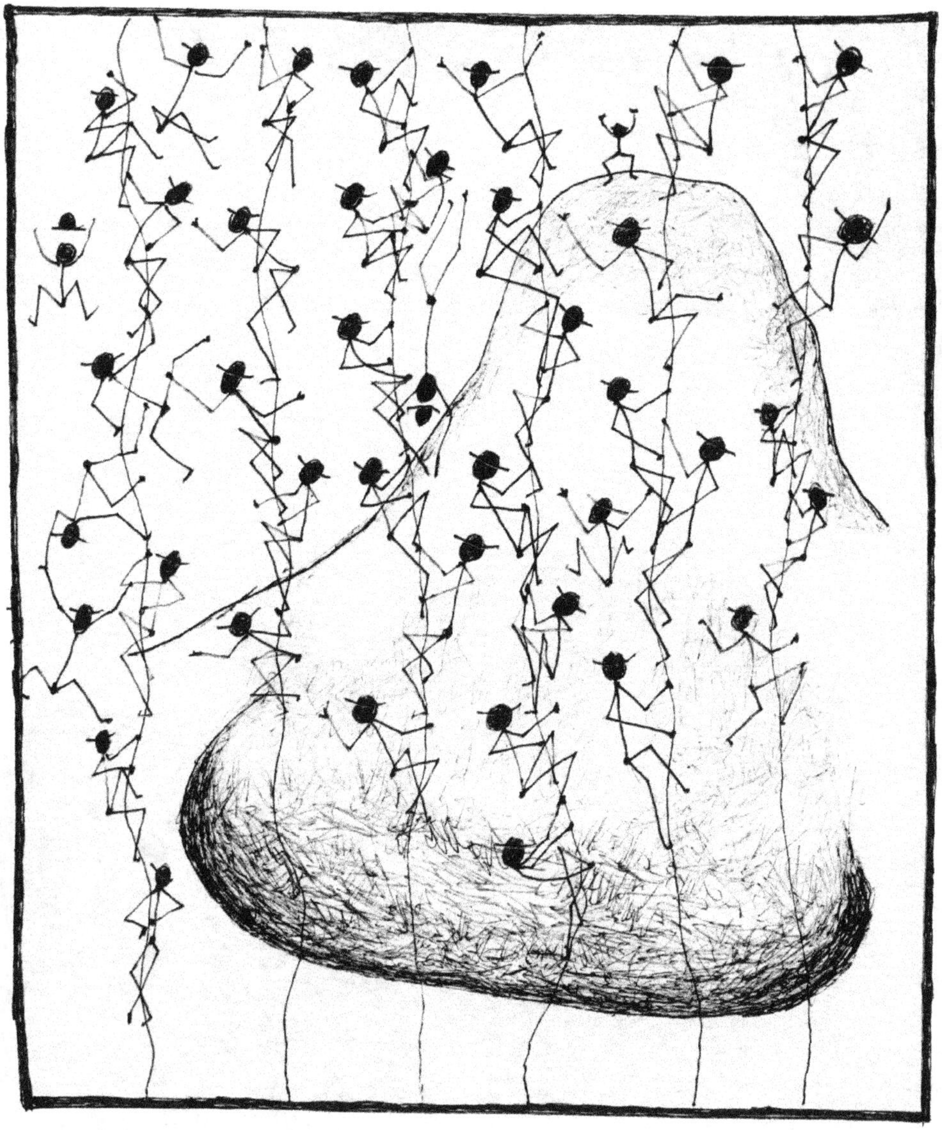

Fourteen: World Night, Black Crystal

World Night
at Black Lake.

Nothing distributed.

Volatility stilled.

Black Crystal.

Volatile particulates
anterior to the Confusion
that otherwise possesses you.

Antithetical parties
dispersed.

Authorities confiscate
magic stones
if they find them.

Volatility enervates
the deep volcanic charge of living Crystal;
hence the termination of all such.

Volatility enervates the Nation;
hence no animation.

Syzygy
claps the lid
on her own blank box.

Incomprehensibility
writes its
own Syzygy.

This text seems odd here.

Wrench Boy
contemplates
the barely legible *scribulariae*
that scratch the stone.

Each Syzygy thinks
a soul in ink
sucked from Black Lake
as if that living well
were but some magic black ink pot.

Broken Presence
wrenches Wrench Boy.

Speech clots Mind
with arid Strength
if World is Night.

Black lakes
work shadow syzygies
through wary treasuries
reduced to indexical capacities.

Whoever receives such missives as this is —
your Volatility gutters
in empty waters.

How does Speech
sink in its own sea?

The cauldron of night
drinks down
the night.

Thought dispersed
in its own Presence.

Improbable determinations
unwrench Wrench Boy.

What present strength must he modulate
to get past this?

Part-thoughts
bleed out.

[]

Long River
weathers Happenstance
in front of The Old Hotel.

Absence absents and resumes itself
dispensing with interval.

Authorities
extirpate
the colored stones.

Have forever done this.

.

How does Strength
get through this?

Night becomes Black Crystal.
Its particulates resume the Volatile.

Hammerhead is born again
out of his own *spoon.*

To every thing apparently visible,
its own Black Box.

[]

A patina
of sentience
combs Presence.

Melee's wont
is to wait.

The Present as such
arranges its referent
to X-out Black Lake.

Volatility's
indices
trouble normalcy's.

Do you see an engine here?

Black Lake articulates.

Volatility
takes off
from your Opal.

You sit on your box
and recur to Black Lake.

[]

Eventuality adjudicates History. Naturally.
One would say that.
Two Jaguars
to each
specious moment: two leaps.

But there is One Wrench Boy (only) —
one to an episode.

One Melee.

Melee keeps her eye
on the Nation
waiting for a Black Globe to crack
and the polity to codify
disjunctive Heredity.

Presiding justices
addle the precedents,
enforcing federations of bewilderment,
not re-wilderment.

The Old Hotel emerges AS World Night.
Lights go on at one window, out at another.
The big house blinks in the mist.
The tune-type of Long River —
nobody's music.

Fragility hugs the Volatile —
Absence is epochal.

Black Lake proclaims the release
of the Syzygies' Bedlam.
They zoom
to high zones.

Stability sufficient to maintain
a measured Melee —
then Violets.

The Syzygy for Wrench Boy
(just this time)
as volatile as an
economy of mercury.

Though an army of African Rattles
would mock the Intelligible, The Intelligible
is incorrigible,
stone-walls the Rattles,
and Will Not be Mocked.

Its Volatility is sufficient for Wrench Boy
to travel fresh *gno-emes*
gorged up from Black Lake.

He can do this . . .

Interval

heart muscle
shuffles blood
awkwardly

suspended
in the social nexus

then
dispersed

a bird with two heads
gold feathers streaked sable
on the shoulders
of a man
with no face

Black Lake appears in the gap
that opens in your aura
if you see that bird.

I see him
talking
modestly
among friends.

Then he vanishes.

I am friendly
to the children
in the villages —

then off for the jungle bodegas with tin roofs
to buy preparatory substances.

Fifteen:
Epistemic Threats

Melee pursues hereditary
Incomprehensibility.

Why?
Whither?

Wherever
Hammerhead
leaves his littered trail.
Shards and angry hammerings.

Incomprehensibility
politicized.
You try to hide it.
They all do.
We all do.

The sound of an African Rattle?
Anthropological.

We inherit
the honed thoughts
of the established intelligentsia,
no matter that, brought to a proper
comparison with our own,
perhaps incompetent, data,
they prove Incomprehensible.

Hammerhead dances over
his own Incomprehensibility.
That's one mood he has.

We, however, choose
solicitous quietude
and bide our Opal,
when Absurdity renders The Grid.

Wrench Boy is with us.

Black Lake is accessible
ubiquitously, if but for a vanishing moment,
and to Wrench Boy
and through him
to all of us.

Who are we?

[]

Some Jaguars are invidious sorcerers.
Wrench Boy tames them
with instruments devised
to make appropriate adjustments
in each one of us —
but quietly — you might not notice this.

But then there is Melee
peeking in at the window
or peeking out. Which?

Melee
intimated
in the afternoon's
meteorological assessment —
or in our hereditary Disposition (Dispossession)
as read off by appropriate
Asclepian authorities — information
distributed liberally
across the home terrain, terrestrial or somatical.

[]

Suddenly there were Jaguars everywhere —
armed
on mission from the heliport —
the Fragility of our situation
recognized by those
poised to take heed, not ourselves; Melee
in general
to be deterred,
it being the concern of the fire-chiefs
to sit on her potentiality
for pharmacological insurgency.
            Wrench Boy,
however, manifests
only in shadows. He is well-protected
by a studied disinclination
to countenance too determinate a registration
of his own being here.

He keeps
his rooms unnumbered
at The Old Hotel.

Others' numbers
surround them.
They are situated in formulae
incomprehensible to all
but those initiate
in the dissolving
grounds of the plausibility
that all numbers are unique and well-confined.
They are not.

If you understand this
you too will tend
to disconsolate heredoms
and render yourselves well-disposed
to Melee and her energies.

Energies such as hers
are not thought subject
to Heredity. Formless
forces
ought not be orderly,
in spite of the weather mathematics,
nor can they be distributed
in successive sites
over time.
        But Jaguars —
live ones — race
across the no-osphere —
as majestic, epistemic threats
lurking underneath and in
and through these
mind-like jungle tangles.

[]

Existence itself is ontologically fragile
and peculiarly distributed.
There are gaps and hollows,
holes and liminal regions
where the Jaguars vanish
on the instants they're descried,
and you cannot say what is and what is not.
Stability
under such conditions
becomes
a political desideratum.

Identity denied
spawns
identity.
There are laws
against radical
intelligence
prioritized
in flagrant agendas.

[]

Who controls whom here?

Can Existence itself
emanate a Syzygy?

Certainly
Wrench Boy
will not declare himself on that one.
There are matters, he avers,
whose determination is ill-suited to promote
our proper *extro-gression*.

[]

Strength, in white linen,
is not dispersed
by Melee's radical distribution
of her willfulness
at sites along Long River,
sites themselves
liberally distributed.

[]

We are speaking on the scale of a Nation,
neither planetwise
nor that of the observable universe
nor radically small,
and indeed there are entities
to whose effective reach
scale is never pertinent.

Power itself
is Volatile
until adjusted by Wrench Boy.

He might, on occasion,
don the very being of some Hammerhead;
augment Happenstance;
effect extraordinary calls or eerie songs
as if to a mystic lover across Black Lake.

Strength herself in white linen,
whose lion becomes a black Globe —
Incomprehensible only if Ubiquitous
force fields fail to exhibit their gaps.
Incomprehensible only
if Black Box lid-like fixtures are ripped off
and black Crystals disperse black light
and all thought is altered or sapped
or proffered in erratic regions, Incomprehensible.

Ubiquity itself is Incomprehensible,
Confusion distributed universally.
But Crystal drives coach and horse
over Melee's regimen of tornadoes,
and incomprehensible itineraries of Jaguars
render the route
even of Long River
Incomprehensible.

[]

What is
Presence?

(Notice: Ontological Regime Change: Presence is Back!)

That
before which
even Black Lake
is a tease . . .

Master Jaguar
is radically stable,
though the Strength that wells up
in his jungle avatars
renders his epistemic regime
Incomprehensible.

[]

I practice my diet of Violets—
a regimen to accommodate Black Lake,
disperse the accouterments of human form and habit
lest that which is Incomprehensible *here*
and progenitive of
cognitive Melee
seem so even *there*
in the precincts of Black Lake
where Absence is rich and salutary
and the practice of the human realm
is itself
Incomprehensible.

Sixteen:
Ubiquitous Particulates

Crystal's stable office
depends upon the Absence
of Violet's Ubiquity.

One plane of apparency
exchanges with another.

Magical experiments
performed
in a proverbial Black Box.

Stability generally
exchanges with Ubiquity.

Violet is always *somewhere.*
Yet this property of hers
never obviates absence.

One must not be confused by this.

The provenance of such an operation
is almost in another world
from Jaguar's — or Melee's, for that matter —
but not quite.
Long River connects all things,
all strenuously segregated regionalities.

There is a Jaguar possible,
whatever the Happenstance.

Jaguar circumambulates
the crystallographer's inquiry.
The exchange of ordered particulates
comprises his crystal's
metastability anyway.

Heredity is operative
within the pertinent "group."

Happenstance furnishes
contextual particulates
requisite for the Presence of Crystal,
who stands outside
the laboratory office,
the very picture of fascination,
Jaguar glancing at her
as he paws a massive black Globe.
Who *is* she, really?

Now, the Ubiquity of particulates
within the Crystal
will not induce stabilization,
unless hereditary patterning —
the work of certain "animate" but non-human persons —
animate Happenstance.

The presence of the hereditary principle is mysterious —
an operant material is not yet a principle —
like a sorcerer's hand
making passes over Happenstance.

[]

Wrench Boy commissioned the operation
and pretended to perform it.

He flushed an avatar
with a profusion of Violet tincture;
imbibed a massive gob
of black tobacco juice;
became first parrot then Jaguar;

prowled Black Lake without moonlight;
mimed with perfect accuracy
the vast, crepuscular, phonic
insect and riparian
density, impossible not to attend to
in that region;
and established an invisible Ubiquity.
Violet was thus apparent Anywhere
without having to manifest Everywhere.

[]

What about that black Globe?

Innumerable small holes
ruined its sphericity
but, inverted, each hole itself
became a Globe,
its Heredity invariant across inversion —
the tiny globes, molecular members
of a fragrant, atmospheric mass —
a Nation of olfactories
comprising sharp, if fragile,
discriminable elements.

[]

I can't see.
My right eye is running
with the intensity of the thought
beneath its unexceptionable survey.
If I exchange it
for the ordinarily inoperant left one,
will it reduce
the Incomprehensibility
of this discourse?

[]

First of all,
it isn't discourse.
It isn't even writing, exactly.
Connect the dots and see what you think.
Say it with what pleasure in the business you can muster;
keep certain salient idealities operant
but with but
a minimum of calculation;
perform this as an act
in the material and social mass
among which you perform *yourself.*

What do you call that?

[]

It is his practice both to mock
and exaggerate Stability.

His Ubiquity is positively riverine.

Who is *he*?

My *own* dalliance with Ubiquity is inalienable —
a condition which, together with contingent availability
induces me to pick up my African Rattle
and take to the pleasure rooms
of The Old Hotel —
the deuce with Stability.

[]

What sort of responsibility is it
to say one is a Nation?

[]

Happenstance is, perhaps,
inalienably Volatile
but metastable;
and if you take into account its higher register,
functionally Ubiquitous.
It doesn't become something else:
it is already, at every point and nexus,
precisely by virtue of being only *here,*
indomitably Elsewhere.

[]

Hammerhead suddenly became cognizant
of the figure of Strength.
A Melee in Hammerhead's intelligence.

The crystalline particulates configured by his spirit
distributed themselves in a new way.

Happenstance, for him,
entered its most volatile phase,
and the figure in white linen
opening the jaws of the lion
looked like nothing at all
but an unintegrable Melee.

Happenstance: a fire truck screaming
its maniacal self-important signal
in front of a house
a few doors down,
no fire
sensible
anywhere.

Violets all aflutter.
My heart muscle
shuffles blood
awkwardly.
The fire-workers
in full regalia
do not seem materially concerned.
Go and see what's happening.
Cat in a treetop?
False alarm?
No facts forthcoming.

[]

I
am responsible
for everything.
That's what an "I" is.

The syzygy of Melee
with or without hereditary postulates
conducing to the metastability of Crystal.

[]

If Ubiquity
ever came over Hammerhead . . .

Well it did.

The Confusion
that clouds
every Opal.

The Confusion
at the bottom
of Volatility.

The general ontological
subvention of world and rumor —

The Confusion!

Seventeen: Money Has An Enemy

"If you don't have any money,
you're junk.
Period.
Into the gorge with you,"
fretted Hammerhead.
His volatility index
zoomed.
Where had all the money gone?
Down Long River's
invidious meanderings.
No Syzygy or paramour
to recover it,
no Black Lake restore.
Volatility
fluxed
Long River.

"Where is my Syzygy," he moaned
as the morning blared
its vigorous sunlight,
"down in Deep Storage
where my Africas languor?
I rattle Happenstance
exhaustively,
but no opportunity knocks at me.
I'd barter my crystals if I had any.
If you don't have money, you're junk
and huddle alone
in sordid chambers —
if some old old old
old hotel
will provide them.
O Happenstance, deliver me;
bring Strength, but better bring MONEY!
I am Hammerhead!
I stand on the brink!

I once owned the bank!
Hammerhead needs no Volatility —
he is stable, and Strength
is *his* to distribute —
Hammerhead the Happenstance Maker,
the Rigor of the Nation.
Oh why has Long River run by me?"

Hammerhead sat by the lip of the gorge
and attempted to tamp down Volatility,
but the thing took the form of a weasel
grown in his own maw.
It slinked about and bit him
and would not go stable.
His grievous monologue
would have to run on a bit longer.

"What is Strength
when the money's gone —
fiduciary capacity itself,
down to the last doubloon, the bottom drachma,
ransacked and redistributed;
Stability invisible;
Strength Incomprehensible.
That which is Stable
is locked in a vault
under The Old Hotel
like some senile border's sack of cash in storage,
a Black Box against Confusion.
Why didn't I stash one back in the day? . . .

"But Happenstance is only Happenstance,
no higher register to it
when Fragility only
is what Long River delivers me.
If you have no money . . .

death with no sequelae.
My ankles are swollen,
my calves are like bricks,
my sons are on furlough
from filial duty. . ."

[]

Jaguar had nothing to contribute
in the way of syzygetical compensation
or other anodyne.
"When Happenstance rattles up a melee," he considered,
"you abide.
Metastability only pertains to The Old Hotel.
Fabricate levels?
Abdicate Heredity?
Exist without time?
Pass into your Opal?
That which is Incomprehensible merely
may open upon the Enigmatical.
This would require an operation
upon the very precincts of speech.
My Crystal is nestled
in the fur of my left fore-paw.
My Opal enfolds me.
Thus turn I from the tease and terror
that Existence is.
I pretend no Syzygy;
the Absence of the which
educes my Stability.
But I *have* The Old Hotel,
its architecture is like Crystal,
black Globe in the foyer
and who shall crack it?

Metastability *be* my opal.
That which I *say*
shall be sufficient Syzygy.
I take out my African Rattle
and enter upon Study.
Violets collect on the roof beams."

[]

Crystal reserves her Strength
and maintains her Presence.
Stability is not
qualification
but result.
The Incomprehensible
contains itself
if one is sensible
to the Volatile.
We know we too are Hammerhead,
inherently prone to depletion.
Wrench Boy
keeps to his Crystal,
furtive, metastable,
depleted in *one* of his forevers
far down Long River.

Interval

The toad doctor
rode in on the vine.

We ate him.

He reappeared before us
in an oily vapor
that shined with a sordid, foggy light
interspersed with crystalline scintallae, very pure,
irregularly spaced and rising
into the over-hanging jungle tangle
as if to give report
of distant and otherwise
invisible
celestial phenomena.

The toad thing lectured:

"You must cease these abstractions,
supplant fragility, stability
with little stones and stars;
volatility
with pot, cup cat's bowl, chalice, cauldron,
but stated singly, not *ad seriatim*.
That will fix you.
I hope I shall not have to come again."

There appeared a pot of black iron
and the toad leapt into it.
The fog cleared.
The jungle became full of sounds, very mirthful.
One had the sense
that back of the vast black tangle
the stars came out.

Eighteen:
All The Young Philosophies

Violet wraps her pearly tendrils 'round
The Incomprehensible,
and above the single turret
ascending from the Old Hotel's north porch,
one star portends an opening
onto stellar punctilliae: each point
one thought.

In a flush:
a fragrance of May flowers,
and Wrench Boy awakens,
on the green lawn
that covers the hill called "Primaeval."

The Old Hotel
shall be housing
a grand confabulation
of ontologies
articulable and non —
attitudes and arguments —
propositions and postures –
a melee of possibilities, unexceptionable,
neglected, or unthought yet,
together with prompt responses
to otherwise incomprehensible deliverances,
each room
one thought.

It is not at all certain whether Wrench Boy
will be able to sustain
his primordial posture.
That Hill is not to be ascended.
And if you *do* ascend it,
against the edict that pretends
it cannot be accomplished,

you do become invisible.
Invincible.
Invisible.

The Old Hotel, if no one else, is happy.
Wrench Boy emits an avatar which
to attend the proceedings, descends,
weakening in intellectual probity,
as his invisibility
declines from him.
He can do nothing but supply unexceptionable summaries
and apt elaborations
of propositions and positions which,
if interdicted yesterday,
are entertained presently as
more or less workable.

Philosophies thus are vigorously projected
in all their articulate varieties.
Everything is happening.

The Old Hotel rolls out the carpet
for ten thousand "Jacks" from Black Boxes.

Hammerhead is skeptical.
Yet the inclusiveness of the occasion
proves irresistible. Who would be left out
from the catalogues of Everything?
He casts about the Globe
for some semblance of a precedent,
and finding indeed such a "semblance,"
thinks to contribute his voice,
it being of a Strength incontrovertible,
a veritable cauldron of aptnesses.

Meanwhile a strong and parallel Violet
propagates violets.

Incomprehensibility takes on
a sort of materiality
in the form of an inhuman Person
clothed in starlit raiment
holding a Big Cup.

Where thinking covers Being, Imagery,
theorized,
slinks
among.

"What shall become of our hereditary appointments?"
she wonders. And violets trickle
over the marble
rim of the thing she
grips strongly in the thing
that must be her hand.

An opalescent Globe
is rising in it,
and The Old Hotel
fills up with pungent smoke.

We take a whiff
and turn violet.
Dizziness quivers.
Incomprehensibility
is a goddess now,
quite because each thing
and every thing
that can be understood
has adequately been so.

She opens her arms in a double arc across us
and little tinsel star points
jump from the cat's bowl
that lies
        cracked and slightly smelly
on the carpet. Hereditary stars point,
but inherited from what exactly?
Surely not the furnaces of hydrogen
filling the cup of cosmic cosmicness
astronomically ubiquitous
in the epoch that succeeds "recently."

But should this
benign profusion
of Good Ideas
implicate Infinities
greater than the meager
transfinite cardinalities
that structure The Old Hotel,
Black Lake and its jaguars can be accessed
from any *point* in it.

Hammerhead checked himself
when his calculations found those twinkling objects.

"Fishy. Very fishy.
My Syzygy has no requirement
of twinkling spiculates. Violet
must quiet down.
When May goes June and beyond that
all too soon
rich summer fades,
a different distribution of anagogic tokens
shall percolate from Black Box,
a single object now.

"Let all these *children, these philosophies,*
find their stones,"
says Hammerhead,
"and begin to know their Syzygies.
Meanwhile,
I'll read their books."

[]

Violet crept
down along Long River,
and the stars
withdrew
behind the fog of proliferate ontologies.

Wrench Boy
took out his Opal
and kept company with Violet.

"Let Strength
return
to Happenstance,"
he whispered,
"Confusion be licit and dispersed.
The Old Hotel is like an Opal
in which a veritable
Nation of young philosophies
finds its voices —
such is the present geography of our no-osphere,
and The Old Hotel
is exorbitantly occupied.

"Well, here's a cup to our young contemporaries, dear Violet.
They do not consider that Crystal extends
the local occupation of what such thinking
cannot recognize as Now, for though Now
is not only Now,
it is never Then,
and needs no reconciliation
among The Stars,
whose indices show Strengths
that well might be quite
indecipherable.
The Old Hotel is not
a cosmos, these days, dear Violet,
but a meager dot
upon a globe,
one star
above its broken turret,
African Rattles,
invisible African Rattles,
their sounds full of stellar punctilliae,
a cauldron in the basement,
of The Old Hotel,
and an Opal
on the mantle
in the foyer,
an opalescent Presence —
the Old Hotel itself,
very smoky."

Then the smoke dispersed,
and this palace of philosophies
returned to its latent percolations
through the rooms and lounges
and hidden corridors
of the Old Hotel
whose quiet prepossession
was not in the least
ironical.

Nineteen:
The Factory

Two of them. One
in the attic,
one very long
in the jowls.
It would be
a stretch
to connect them, yet
they hang together
as in a magisterial abstraction —
a grand rotunda
where a chandelier
glitters
from the would-be abject sunlight
trenchantly invading
thought space.
A "sphere" of fractioned light, actually.

These gods are not our gods,
but they cling
to the inner circle . . .

a black puddle
at the bottom of everything
where the cat's bowl tinkles
in the indigo twilight from the rain.

Your Nation is not my nation:
obviously this obviates polity,
yet there is a cauldron
where the local people congregate
to assert a sort of pedigree, a Presence —
an enormous pot of disparate objects.
Nobody knows how it got there
or where they themselves
had arrived from,
but that they had had a bad journey
traveling in twos —

diploid wanderers in Obliquity —
Incomprehensibility was their comfort —
just that they were there
among stones
and double-handled chalices —
a sort of proto-sentience
among the beings of the microscape —
there was no Confusion, really —
the Globe and its variegated twin splinters of star-night in the small —
the vast absences that haunted the *mise en scène* —
the lack of desire
to solve the Incomprehensible —
the present moment
was a place
where no decision waited
to determine itself
through you —
each moment
was like a vivid stone
apart
even from the perquisites of mystery —
in that sense very bright, very clean —
and then the Giant just assembled itself
with his trumpet
where the grand river
ran
beneath the second story window . . .

[]

Strength
was the subject
of Africa
and its crackling,
storm-riven
afternoons —
what did it smell like?

Why ask that?

It smelled like an epidemic
of big house cats
on another continent.
They paired off and together surveyed the sounds
they found themselves composed of —
two beat units —
two unit houses—
incomprehensible utilities
among the rags and cornices
from beneath which they literally flew up
to settle on the tops of cabinets
out of reach
and then the snow . . .

[]

There was an abandoned factory
filled with potshards
and *hundreds* of cats —
each one a micro-consciousness —
but their collectivity was unimaginable —
starry patterns pointing
through dusty fur,
pcbs
from the stagnant
industrial blue
pools where the cement
drank . . .
huge cracked crystals
hanging from heavy rusted
chains—
the corporate entity
that eventually
would inherit the place
had not been established at that time.

[]

A strange boy
who lived tenuously
in the shack
on the cliff side
above the ruins —
"Cat Boy" the locals called him —
searching for his sister
and she
was watching the cats
but had the trick of invisibility
only before him —
to all others
she could not *ever* be witnessed —
the cats' eyes were so dull —
a violet dye
spilled
across their windshields.

What was dispensing
the deleterious liquids
with such adamant ferocity?

A cracked black globe
occupied a flat landing
where twin, deflated dirigibles
had settled
in their final phase.

[]

Be quiet if you want to avoid confusion?
That's always advisable.
Why? Because stillness
attracts the "true" Now

from which no decision
requires anything of you.
You are awake
and Hammerhead
can't see you
even if he's right there —
the state of your being is incomprehensible to him
as is his
to *you,* actually.

You might be holding an African Rattle.
You may have realized the Syzygy
or transferred your entire psychic physiognomy
into a glowing orb.
It doesn't matter.

Cat Boy
is holding his own orb now
and *that* matters
to the situation
because no chaotic stress
or incomprehensible residues
will distort his attitude
which has to twin your own,
if together
you will stretch Happenstance
to its bottomless apogees
where violets
and madder bluetts
and portulaca blossoms
proliferate
in the dusts
of broken industry.

[]

What you say then
will not be Incomprehensible,
to me at least —
there are necessities
to utterance
which follow their own grooves.

[]

Two strange boys now
are sitting on chairs
looking fixedly
into the black puddle.

They are protecting a secret
by inducing unsociable mind states
with incommunicable depths,
and the two boys
unbeknownst to their own Syzygies
are committing their being
to intensities
yet to come over them —
years later perhaps —
by the cool and practiced waters
of Black Lake.

Twenty: The Grand Concordat

A shadow
passed
into the underground
awakening imperial anxiety.
Random access
to the prince's porches.
The fire-chief's headdress —
red helmet with white feathers.
You turkey.

The little people leap on the rooftops
welcoming the sound of great water,
the roiling clouds
compounding national self-approbation.

Rigor attacks clutter, clutter, rigor.
Clatter clatter.

The fire-chiefs write their own rules;
but even these
gatherers of squalid sovereignty
are ignorant of conditions
invisibly gathering
along the river-gutters.
They command their own presence
but see double.

[]

I don't witness particulars
but assess the ambience
from its noise,
its pulse,
its smell.

Musn't grumble.
Hide my Opal.

One doesn't blurt out
the ratty potentialities
that lurk about
indecipherable apparencies.

So much for "Presence."
But it has your back.

[]

The pertinent ideation
is distributed liberally
among persons
variously concentrated,
variously instrumentalized —
workers
obliged by their rivers
oblivious and sad —
only a confrontation
of absolute candidates —
candidates for the recrudescence
of The Configured Absolute —
preparation for the Grand Concordat
among sovereigns
from diverse ontological companies —
the addled fire-chiefs
for whom the other candidates
are not weird enough,
the stellar objects
and their coded designations
stunned
with a remote familiarity.

[]

If you think
what can be thought,
you circumscribe the Nation
and become the local Thinker
who distributes little books
to the Species Captains.
Cosmology is the enemy:
a burly fellow
whose real name is Absence
checked into The Old Hotel.

The fire-chiefs are nowhere
to receive your obeisance.
You stand before the National Cauldron
where what happens
happens without Obliquity
and yet the excess
that is What Is —
not even a Black Box
can possibly stand in for.
Stars perhaps
whose interior bottoms
are indefinite
from any other's point of view
but for themselves
no distribution
manages the variables.
You see a Crystal
hanging in the direction of endeavor
but then it is gone
and the Nation remains
as its shadow, its revenant.
Wrench Boy
works the melee,

shapes a new Globe
again
again
again
again
again
a national Black Box
is promulgated —
everybody sees it.
It spins
on a bottom corner
when the young boys toy with it
knocking their little wrench heads
against its faces
to see if they can identify
in the hollow sound
respondent, the objects
in there
that may prove discernible
from indentations, discontinuities,
blanks, in the sound field, you must attend
the echo, not to locate
but to *know*
if violets
proliferate
instead of blanks
in the algebra
and big cats
show themselves
from whatever continent they come out of
probably Africa; if Violets
proliferate
instead of Absences
in the echo field
and jazzmen
keep it going
as distraction, misdirection,

so no one notices
just what is missing
from the mind space—
Wrench Boy
assumes another head—
this one
spectacularly elaborate box stacks
formed to *look* like a head
(roughly like a head)
and the little
national people
on the roof tops
enthuse
when they sense his Presence
and he allows
his African Rattles
to come back
from stony silence
from the Absence
that had inhabited them
while they renegotiated their vitality—
they'd gone off
to their twins
in Obliquity
for that purpose —
Wrench Boy also away
with red-freckled Melee.
Confusion is a good thing
mustn't grumble
Deep Storage
revivifies through Absence —
the Nation
will have another life
on a different Globe,
Jaguars surmount
the Incomprehensible,

Black Box
open wide
on a Black Lake
that is like
a black lake . . .

INTERVAL

Jacinth troubled the pot.

The cement factory fell in the sea.

America all table cloths and strawberries.

Heart space filled up with bubbles.

Sleep necessary, not welcome.

Dawn rain.

The doctor
sat on the vine.

Toad below
the stacked boxes.
Where is Crystal?
Where is the sun?

Desire distracted, misdirected.

Cat Boy sat on the rim
of the blue cistern
dropping empties.

Gravity is like a sorcerer's passes
over the archetype of cities.

An hour before dawn
the buildings don't think of the sun —
their towers
obliviate the sky.

A little child
with a prickly beard

keeps notes on it.

Where is my list of word tokens —
my pattern,
my monkey bars?

The cat stays away all day,
where was she?

Under the cornice
on top of the chest
hidden
in her own happy shadow.

Now she's back and wants
my complete attention. Why?

Is it possible to scrutinize
the intelligence of a cat?

She's a damaged being.
A broken history.
Does she know that?
Can she remember
the blue fluids,
the mortal vats
of ontological cement?

Am I Cat Boy?

Should I stare in a puddle?

Where is my double, my exegete?

When will they come to remove my Outer Man
and give me back my —

white stone,
my quiet morning.

Jacinth remains at large —
here is her cauldron, unattended.

When will the money . . .

Twenty-One: The Visitor

The land below
has no sign of big cats,
no building complex,
no monumental stones.
What we did sense
was a strong whiff of something untoward
rising from under the handsome stand of oak trees,
so we descended to take a look.
There *were* stones down there
hidden by the foliage,
and the only way I can put this
will not be easily credited.
The odor was a massive intensification
of the smell of *life itself.*
Teaming, intricate, sentient, moribund life.
And the smell had a color, and a kind of translucence
as if of wildly attenuated Violets.
And there *were* some buildings —
very small but inhabitable
with all the necessary facilities:
aqua-synthesizers, atmosphere
filtration systems, gravitational
concentration devices — gadgets
for quieting the various unhappy
sensations and other
qualifications of sentient states
to living species general.
The compound was in fact
the housing arrangement
for the Species Captains.
Each kept an Opal.

I mentioned all this is my report
and signed it, attaching
the appropriate fragments of smashed crystals
that can only be purchased with the Truth —

my allotment of the latter
being diminished thereby.
I have had a lot of trouble
getting my narratives validated,
I can tell you that. As one's allotment
runs out,
one's own faith in what one has uttered
diminishes accordingly.

[]

Cat Boy had returned to the station
after his interment at the abandoned cement factory.
He of course had no recollection
of having spent
moments in so imaginally provocative a setting —
only fragmentary affective
flashes — just enough
to stimulate a slightly queasy
feeling of confusion —
a certain distrust of the probity
of the present *mise-en-scène* —
a sense, that is,
that the elements of existence
might have been assembled with some haste —
that the connectivity
twixt one moment and its sequel
had been haphazardly arranged —
that perhaps one wasn't Cat Boy
or Cat Boy "uniquely"
but — and this was the uncreditable thing —
there suddenly appeared an edifice
whose chambers manifested
now as vast and elegant,
now as a motley of — how to say this —

too many worlds — each shoved up close
against another.
There were signs of stress at the contact points
and the sound — first from far away,
then on-coming, then roaring
all about one's ears —
of a giant river; then
in the next instant —
but the next instant was a gap;
and in it
one knew who one was:
not a definite personality, identity, sense of filiation,
nothing like that; but as if the Veils
of Incomprehensibility had lifted
and there one stood
a handsome Jaguar
with spats, I mean spots,
and full feline capacities,
intelligent and energetic —
not like a still small point
at which one was what one was,
but an open sky beyond self-hood —
not a black box, indefinite and sequestering,
but gemlike, spacious, sometimes smoky,
sometimes pellucid or radiant, always happy,
always deep, always wise.

[]

Jaguar stepped off the *mise-en-scène*
and resumed the management of The Old Hotel.
It had a certain timeless character to it,
as it always had
in the autumn
when the river — it had a name
but no history —

was full and happy.
The point is: it was that body that
appointed moments to their
antecedents and sequelae
so that the incomprehensible gaps
that actually *were* these moments —
their positive qualities came in from intransitive elsewheres —
Long River saw to that —
so that the gaps themselves
would subtract the Absence of Heredity
and the nature of existence itself
seem like a Globe.

[]

The Vandals
were in Africa,
then they weren't.
That's an instance.

The sound of the epoch
was distributed
among the small
surviving stones.
They have a certain Presence
with stellate configurations
that are not only on the skin of the stones
but deep
causing Hammerhead
as was his wont
to distrust Happenstance.
He hated it in fact.

There is an avatar of Hammerhead
that despises the exigencies of the extant:
the used bowls of oatmeal
and the strawberry residues;
the empty goblet of false milk
when cinnamon particles
stick to the sides;
and the spoon—
he hates his own spoon —
it clinks as the wash water vanishes
and it settles on top of the drain;
and the agitations of laundry;
counting money;
humiliation before that
chubby cute teller
at the bourse
and her crucifix lackadaisically dangling;
tasks at the combustion chariot;
the traffic; the advertence
to irrelevancies, then
to necessities,
to one's person —
all this — better make it go away —
and the True Work
of one's True Nature —
occupy and exhaust one
till boredom or languor
inaugurate slumber —
then arousal —
then work again.
There's an avatar of Hammerhead
who is like this —
and it explains a lot . . .

[]

All does not quite proceed
as if nothing existed
outside the Crystal;
but Heredity works like contagion,
identity spread across silence,
prowling jaguars
about an old hotel
where no one abides anymore
but they've left their Opals
to Happenstance
which is what *is* outside,
but inside too, that's the trouble,
and Long River flows both ways,
so it's useless as explanation —
a melee in the mind
depends upon the consistency of your Opal
as to whether it addles ontology
sufficiently
to allow you to experience the truth
that you are ineliminably at one
with Happenstance
and that the Higher Register of the latter
is like a Black Lake.

It sits in a chalice —
never mind the size.

Once Wrench Boy drank down Black Lake.

If your syzygy introduces you instantaneously
to your True Nature —
your stash of Verity is replenished.
You have access to the deep deep pockets
where that currency is deposited.

The distribution of Truth
is a function of Wrench Boy.
There is no Higher Happenstance
but that you take the High Road, the High Tone,
and the grand and empty sky
shall cover the Nation
finally —
Black Lake
in the end
quiet the African Rattles
not peremptorally
but ringed round by sentinel jaguars
accoutered so elegantly . . .

[]

If you keep on making
"the same mistake twice"
about Heredity —
it handles the distribution
of temporal particulates.
They come in and pop up
like Violets out of Obliquity —
all the interesting stuff is just like that —
out of Black Lake —
by now a fixture in the mind
but God forbid it should be like that —
it is only Black Lake because it ought never to be like that —
an orb inhospitable to entities
not in some sense avatars of Wrench Boy
and for whom Black Lake and that alone
remains its only Strength.

Twenty-Two: Weirdlings and Wastrels

I know what's happening
here, anyway
on the porch
where the great globe spins
by its own current
with such equanimity
you'd think to be confused
were as remote as that cosmic chalice
said to contain the void
beyond the dyad
behind the world.

But confusion hides
in every chalice: the bubbling
spring of conundrums
Hammerhead inherits
from his own deep mind's
antipathies.

My Jaguar purrs beside me — my Peruvian figment —
that *I* inherit
from my own transformed
antipathies
along with my magic stones
out of the range of blear authorities,
the repositories — the stones that is —
inheritors of the magic
that is Happenstance itself, the ring
of contingency
that marks Tornado Island
off from the fjords and canyons
of ancestral glories
that would bind *that* glory
with realized exigencies
of values long achieved.

Therefore do I keep my Globe
quietly turning
on the porch of The Old Hotel
I built long ago
and in which I install myself
and my magic stones
oblique *to*
yet suffused *with*
all Happenstance.

[]

It was Monday, back a week —
one does inherit the calendar
with its useful if puerile delineations —
Black Lake has no
days and weeks; its Confusion
bubbles forth Happenstance *undelineate*
like my Globe
without holes or edges;
like a well-rounded sphere;
like a heart without warbling or tremor;
like a silent stone
that absents itself
to the central vault
beneath The Old Hotel —
One stone
to replace
the memory of Nations.

[]

I was confused
by the singular Presence
of a swarm of tiny cats —

a melee of miniatures
with little meowling cries
comprising quite an uproar
about my pile of stones.

They wanted me to open the grand oak doors
to my establishment,
not to themselves
but to the Weirdlings and Wastrel spirits
to whom they were affined.
They'd been called
by a vagabond collective
under the sign of a certain stellar cluster
to assemble in front of the doors
while I happened to be there
in a certain affective state
and while Hammerhead
was *not* there.

They indicated
I was to get
one big pot
and set it to boiling,
and when the convection currents formed their cells
just prior to turbulence —
that state when Melee
revels with excitement
at "the edge of chaos"
beyond which
Incomprehensibility reigns —
The Old Hotel would change
and manifest as a Crystalline edifice,
each chamber ensconced beneath a facet,
and the Confusion of discarnate Wastrels
and mental vagabonds

would entrain
to the sounds of an African Rattle that I was to operate
that their spirits might desist
from *their* wonted turbulence.
I would take the form of crone Jacinth.
The Old Hotel would be
like a Nation of Wastrels
returned from Confusion
to their original radiance,
and I would place my stones
in a Black Box,
one stone to a Wastrel;
and they, though this rite
last but a moment,
would have a home forever
in their room
in The Old Hotel;
and though Confusion
reign in their spirit
for its Strength is forever,
the Melee that lives in Black Box
is salutary, generative, a wonderful resource,
a Globe of Life.

[]

I thought I'd built
The Old Hotel
for my own occupancy;
but Wrench Boy came
and amused my Confusion
with rattle out of Africa and Peru;
and Long River receives
whatever Melee
sends through The Nation;

and Jaguar in spats
summons his miniatures;
and there are communities whose spirit
is like Tornado Island;
turbulence is alive in the cauldron
confounding Heredity quite generally;
and whatever occurs,
one has one's Opal
and one's Africa
even if it rattle
in Confusion

and the Confusion
that is not salutary
is eternally deposed.

Twenty-Three: A Further Report from Our Visitor with Remarks on *Telestics*

An avatar of Hammerhead
came out of the strong jungle tangle.

He lectured the Nation
smoking mapacho stogies
or else cachimbo pipe things; stem of bird leg.
Rattles corrupting the suburbs.

His Presence suggested his Africas —
garments so loose and colorful
fluttered to agitate his Wrench Boy —
a National extravagance.

His theme: that you never
lather your body with soap
or luxuriate in hot water bathing
except for magical reasons
lest your Africas
fall off from you.

His Presence was awesome
but nobody possessed
any such Africas
in the precincts that he frequented.

It was a sign of the moment
that he appeared there
in remaining suburban villages —
not actually suburban now
that the cities in all senses had *re-wildered.*

But he liked Tuckahoe
under what once was a rail-bridge
and its prolific stand of willows
no longer green or yellow
but depicted in black and white only.

And on the banks
of Troublesome Brook
now but a parsimonious trickle
— no trouble to come out of it —
so many Violets
out among the stones —
they were the only colored things
inhabiting Happenstance.

Black Box at such times is a secret.
It harbors charged stones and effusions of starnight.

Stones are strong things.
They have a strong nature.
They uphold the Nation
in times
when once there were The Nations.
What are there now?

Globes and stars in grand configurations.

Long *Rivers* are strong.
They pummel stones in an excellent melee.

We all go to Africa
to gather Strength
and make changes in our nature.

If you have a Globe,
it best be a grand one.

These stones pour out like Long River
and the Globe
spins about
among the stars.

That's what I see
in *my* opal.

Interval

Dr. Tongs
came aboard
to examine the unruly rock pile.

He plucked the one
with Jaguar markings
and, for a nanosecond, was afraid.

Of course he soon recovered his professional attitude,
but that nanosecond was enough.
Forever and forever
he would know the stones were alive.

Ontological Volatility in general
was not affected by this.

Things were *already* alive.

But the man was changed:
his lectures allowed strange gaps and shifts;
his prescriptions ingredients unfound
among the pharmaceuticals.

Interval

The Hellenic personage, Daedalus, built statues
that looked like they were alive.

Vitality lies hidden
in one's *metier*:
wood sprite, gem-sprite, Ifrit locked
in bottle, stick, or stone.

Now weird green eyes
gaze out of the god's head,
and the thing is in positive jeopardy
of up and running away.
The devotees and magistrates
put chains to their statues,
and the gods get the message.
They stay
where they
have been made
to stay *put*.

How do you take away life
from an image in stone
once you've *imbued* it
with it?

Avert your gaze
and the green eyes glaze over,
the paint comes off
across the long millennia.

The stone keeps its secrets once again.

[]

[Twenty-three, continued]

Obese operators
of luxury sedans
stop at convenience
outlets
for diverse predictable
articles. I saw them.
I put that in my report.
Why do we want to know such things?
When I initiate inquiry about this,
I stir up a terrible fracas.

There are huge boulders
arrayed in a grand ring
with a village in the middle.
Nobody down there knows why.
I report that also.
Inquiry indicates
that the obese ones take an interest
in the stones
sensing a mysterious presence
in or among them
(to which, by the way, the thin ones
are completely insensible)
often at calendrically significant time points.
You can see them
taking seats
in the great stones' shadows
and putting their fingers
to the surfaces of them.
Something changes in their demeanor
as if a deep confusion
were resolved thereby,

for a moment, anyway,
and they are liberated
from happenstance,
oblique to the demands of the world.
I think I have this right.
I took out rooms
in some old hotel
they have down there
to examine more closely
what they take to be "happenstance."
They think we come from "the stars."
They see us in their "opals."
They remember a "time"
when we were not among them.
But we are clearly here now,
as they themselves withdraw
into the invidious noises
they make with rattles out of Africa
and other objects
hatched from little black globes
available in surprising abundance.
Each globe hatches one object; each object
is capable of emitting
its singular sonority.
And when they come together
for their somnambulist assemblies,
there is a great hall
full of obese people
each with a distinct small machine
for issuing a single utterance.
And in the collective sound of it you have
an impression of the kind of world
there must once have been down there —
interesting harmonies
and crunchy clackings
and grungy barks
and all sorts of clatterings and swishings. I cannot tell you.

At times its seems they come in pairs — duplicates possibly —
and when they are joined in this way,
they emanate an aura of strength
not obvious in the presence of them singly.
And when there are six or seven, or rather ten of them
gathered about a table,
they form a crystal or a force-field
whose quality is like that.

[]

Suddenly, a jaguar became me
(or I him)
and I was unable
to continue my report.
Then, just as suddenly,
Jaguar vanished *from* me,
and joined himself to one of those crystals.

Each node and facet
has one person, none of them
obese any more.
Their association with this
crystal formation
changes their corporeal affinities completely.
Each being holds an opal
which glows
according to the thought
shared by the members in the crystal;
though each being singly believes
her thought derives from "the stars."

What does this signify?
It is not an easy thing to assemble our report.
My mind is a melee.
What do they mean by "the stars"?

Some other sort of "elsewhere"
than our Africa and its Rattles, our Peru —
a purely virtual spatiality devoid of heredity,
or rather so replete with it
that time forms a crystal,
every point and node
fixed towards its own
locally locked-in elsewhere
in our sense, as such?
But I just don't know.

They have a kind of pot
and an object they call
"The Orb of Incomprehensibility,"
to which they allocate all matters
that we know to be real:
stones — but not the obese ones —
while beyond it — well beyond it —
they say they see stars.

To me, The Orb
is like a stone, firm, yet
magisterially rotating,
emitting Happenstance itself —
cats and their cats' bowls,
Jacinth at her cauldron,
fields and fields of little violets,
flowerets and the spirits
associate therewith —
all the things that ought to comprise a world.
But they do not know it that way.

An Entity whose barrows and pockets
just team with mechanical instruments
and all sorts of attitudes,
they metonymize as "Hammerhead,"
lords it over them cantankerously and mightily,

and the violets are forced, though they burgeon,
to manifest abjectly in orderly files and rows.

They do have those things they call "opals"
as accumulators of sentience
and repositories of life,
each violet allowed to consult hers
at such times
as their stars determine.

I swear I don't know why we want to know these things.
Their weird inconsistencies render we who report them
inconsistent as well.
Why not tie them up in a bundle and be done with the disturbance
to our systematic that
their mere presence effectuates?
Next time I visit my Africa
I'll change my nature
and no doubt they'll simply disperse;
meanwhile I must abide
this thing they call "Happenstance,"
being here among them.

In my Africa, what they call "stars"
is Strength Herself,
a woman in white linen,
a Great Red Lion
and so forth.

In Africa,
Being itself
is a small black box.

Twenty-Four: The Cat's Bowl

The cat's bowl as big as
the observable universe
serves a cat
bigger than *it*. That cat
wears an Opal
on a chain
around her black neck
and, regarding what
she might spy
when she puts her eye
to it, we say
what she might see
is like a Black Box. It proffers
that which happens
down below
in the visible world
and much else besides,
we dare not say "all":
no complete distribution
of transfinite worlds
in that Black Box. Thus Jaguar —
for the cat is The Universal Jaguar
and his Opal
that is like a Black Box —
is frustrated somewhat,
incapable of dispersing
everything
through an indefinite world.

She — that is, together with her Syzyzgy —
computes the stellar masses and their spectra —
computation is a kind of Strength —
but the Great Black Lake beyond the stars
guarantees the Incomprehensibility
of many stellate "Everythings,"

but not all of them.
There might be a cauldron
or many cauldrons,
many Opals,
to make up a Nation – call any
incomprehensible ontology
"a nation." Put up a flag,
why don't you,
in front of your Old Hotel.

The point is, whether together
we might situate a chapel,
a black one,
with a perfect chalice
overbrimming with stars.

Go out on any clear June night,
not too humid, the night
is like a black Crystal,
a gigantic cabinet of wonders,
but the earth beneath it
is a big pot — rough red clay,
high-fired, no glaze,
but little shining stones,
agates or opals, incised by the firing.
Out there
you can formulate
an entire Nation of potters, each one
committed
to a kind of consciousness,
however incomprehensible,
to the "everything" that encloses it.
But in the Old Hotel
the old cat manages, well,
a Nation bedecked
with its own Incomprehensibility,
its own self-generated Confusion.

[]

Melee licks baked bricks with her red tongue
and Hammerhead, who is like a supersensible cat,
counts his coppers.

He has a big cup
that exemplifies his overweening Presence.
He has black stones
he keeps in a Black Box
and gives them a toss.
They click and clack
and distribute themselves like black dice
on the checkerboard floor
of an Africa
imagination remembers
from before the great diaspora
of human species
poured out from the lidless
box of a continent —
a melee of bipeds
streaming
out of an angry mother
cauldron
to propagate the nations'
incomprehensible melee —
the nations teaming
with violets.
                    Being
was so happy — Black Lake
upside down
in what looked to everybody like the heavens
defining itself as a Mighty River —
and Hammerhead grumbled
but was happy;

on account of his game of dice
at the gaming tables
of The Old Hotel.
He exchanged the contents entire
of his Black Box for a system of black Globes.
They circulate
in powerful spiratic orbits Incomprehensible —
you have to hide your eyes
when they almost collide in your sight.
They comprise as a system
the Black Crystal of night
the people across the universe
witness as stars.

[]

Wrench Boy sat on his bench
making careful notes —
his forte
was charting the incomprehensible activities
of the Nation
and stashing his observations
concerning Happenstance,
both particular and general,
in a Black Box
to be distributed
when the Mighty Presence
(that could itself take on
any form whatsoever
as far as the people were concerned)
in fact did manifest to each
according to her capacity
to apprehend it.
That's why they said all along
that Being itself
is like a Black Box —

that an absent Hammerhead Incomprehensible —
a Hammerhead aloft
in his own Confusion —
lived with his Great Black Box —
a Mighty Presence
at the root of the world.

Interval: Elsewhere

Jaguar cogitates about a ball of twine.

"The wires and cords and strings
and ropes and tendrils
that spontaneously
and ever-so rapidly
form themselves into a great tangle
of relations and compositions
so that, as a jungle
tangle, they make the appearance
of a world
or a world of worlds —
can only be disentangled
with great deliberateness and attention —
spontaneity being the inverse
of deliberateness and attention —
spontaneous attention, that is, as it were,
turned upside down;

but as the work of untying
the knots and tangles of these
maniacally jumbled
filaments, microtubules, arterials,
and strands
comes to a kind of climax,
the work grows simpler,
and all you have to do is
shake the thing out
and the jungle's clear . . ."

Jaguar cogitates further:

" 'Inhabitants' are enworlded by 'totalities'
constituted as 'Elsewheres'.

"Everything is abstract; that is,
something essential
to a concrete entity
has been deleted in its constitution.

"You can go to a bank
and find it
'on deposit.'
Fragments and particles,
organs and syntagmata:
there they are
in the bank vaults
indexed and secured
and entered on a gigantic ledger.

"There are libraries whose stacks include
nothing at all but these
fantastic codices.

"When an 'Everything' in its universe
reaches a certain phase
or, that is, when the cognoscenti in that locus
come to acknowledge the site
of their totality's absent fragment;
they send an emissary
to the world
that they calculate is inhabited
by that Bank;
for the Bank and its Ledger — its great Red Book —
has the form of a World.

"You don't just *read*
such a book.
You must be inhabited by it;
that is to say,
you must take the form
of a possible 'Elsewhere'

particular to the world
you would be inhabited by
and just so,
come to live there.
                                        Life
is an exchange
of habit: habitudes;
redundancies of actions
forming *things*
that seem
to stay as they are,
while mighty rivers
pass them down their currents
as rocks or boulders,
continents or entire Globes
black or otherwise
rolling in spiratic orbits
impossible to measure
properly
but in some worlds
measured still.

And that's what an 'I' is —
an Emissary to the Bank
sent to scope out a World
in the form of an 'Elsewhere.'"

Twenty-Five: Mind Games

Green frog
covered with goo.

Old institutional
manse   history
blotted.

The predators have gone

to Black Lake
and they sup
on their own
ancestry.
            What happened
in Happenstance
that Friday?

Only Confusion.

Frogs.

Their skin secretes
the most powerful toxins we know. WE?

At Black Lake Lodge
the young zealot searches the ledgers
in the book stacks.

What you denominate "Heredity,"
my pretty one, is
or shall we say "are"?
— No we *shan't* —
suffusions of extracts
from the, do you call them "waters"?
Ha! "Waters" indeed. Would it were so.

People turn into cats
whose ages correspond
to the ages they shed
in being transmuted so. Oh come come —
it's not that Incomprehensible.
You think it's a cat's bowl
and don your shawl.
There's a chill in the air
and a chill, I dare say,
in those waters, stirred up by
paddles and wedges whose handles are nailed on with pegs,
and that, yes that,
is Incomprehensible, I do tell you.

You will not
at the end of it
know who we are.
The traces run backwards,
the foot marks grow dim,
so cease and desist
attempting to put your torch to what
though contextualized temporarily by darkness
are in fact the "flagrant
colors of the indominately so."
You will not change a thing.
What is Present
declares itself
as such
and puts paid
to the excuse
of Confusion.
You know very well if you *will* it.
Otherwise, the Absence of insight,
if it become endemic,
will emanate
all sorts of things.

Your mother came down here
looking for that little black Globe you
brought with you when you
just showed up that night,
for instance.
Do you even have one?
A mother I mean. Now that's
Incomprehensibility for you.
What's my name?
If I tell you,
I'll be Hammerhead.

[]

Magic is sex.
Sex — magic.
Not sex magic.
Not magic sex.

Well, maybe magic sex.
Mind without limits,
mens sine finibus.
That's a motto.
(Any kind of sex.)
My god, how do the images
get in there?
The black green vines,
the great rolling rivers.
If you live with perfect
integral   weave
to the moment, no fuzzed
time edge, to be dead
at the edge . . .
Magic is death,
death — magic.

Death Magic!

Death Sex Magic
at Black Lake Lodge
and the mysterious Presence
of little green frogs,
if they *are* frogs.

They have no "skin."
No one does.
That sheen on their surface.
Why we so urgently
must have that Opal.
Somehow.
By some oblique path.
Some walk around a black Globe.
Forward or back.
You spin it one way,
you spin it the other.
You walk,
walk back.
The Opal appears
out of its own Absence.
Your Absence.
Your obliquity.
Your Africa.
Your rattle.

[]

The road was very straight.
You can see the straight
line   path
between the two bassoons.
The cyclist who carries it
(carries the line, I mean)

is nothing.
Not even breath.
Not even a name.
Just a line.
Between the two bassoons.

[]

The "Poem Itself"?
Nobody wrote it.
The guy is dead, was dead
when he wrote it,
tried to write it;
but the thing to begin with
when he began it
was a Black Box.
Was something in it
but you just don't know quite what?
Or is it the principle of the thing —
the "nothing" itself
was in there,
the condition that cannot be confined
to generate anything —
one thing follows another
and there is a mysterious contagion
between them,
an infection of The Same:
Heredity is comprehensible on those terms
as magic
is as
the casting of images
or the eerie distant
oncoming blank
susurrus
of an African Rattle

all along the Long River
that ambles
under a leaden cloud
through a jungle of Violets
as we amble
obliquely
through a distribution of mind game occurrences.
Is that what you are?
A series of moves in a mind game?
I doubt it.
Everything stops
at Black Lake,
even your mind game.
Mine doesn't.
You are my double, perhaps,
my invert, my complement.
You are absorbed
in Black Lake
while I disguise myself
as a sharp Bank
resplendent with Violets
quite close, I think,
to an Old Hotel.
My Incomprehensibility
might be your Presence
at Black Lake,
a Jaguar Presence
with a proudly
hereditary accumulation
of fists full of Violets,
but I myself
inherit nothing . . .

[]

Crystal naturally
will have nothing to do with this
unless she can cast
her Presence across
the oddly distributed
winkings of starlight
to be seen only now
calmly bright
above a Black Lake
in Africa
that twinkled a long time ago
when we were alternative
hominids but
beginning the business
of our present itinerary anyway —
that prior distribution
of ontological Confusion
was contemporary
with its own form
of Violets
very strong of stem —
you couldn't pluck them —
full of ciliate receptacles, fully circumambient
around Black Lake.

[]

The Nation
was completely invisible,
tucked up
in its own spoon
as big as half a continent.

The thing that was present, most present
about it
was a chaplet of red stones,
opaque ones
incised about the spoon rim,
though one of them was an Opal,
and inside it there lodged the image
that then and now and always
was
Black Lake.

Twenty-Six:
The Kingdom

My mind to me a kingdom is.
No it isn't.
It's a random distribution of seeds
in an African Rattle,
a Melee, really,
a great stony Melee,
strong and terrible, maybe,
but an African Rattle of a Melee,
a stony Melee that conjugates its Jaguars,
that conjures from a position
of oblique Absence,
a veritable Crystal of Obliquity,
a Long River of Absences,
a distribution of genitives,
a dispersion of Africas,
a positive Confusion of misdirected Nations,
a Dispersion of Obliquities,
its Syzygy —
I am still descanting
on the quiddity of my intellect —
its Syzygy is no Melee:
her distribution
is something else,
not in Africa. Peru perhaps.

Universal Confusion
lasts more than this one night,
I can tell you that.
Deep Storage underwrites The Nation
because of this Confusion.
Long River runs through a Black Box.

Alright.
Now YOU tell ME
about what YOUR mind
is
or isn't.

[]

My mind to me
is a bag of stones.

No it isn't.
Violet came in here
with mop and suction device
and dispersed the knocking about
of those pesky dybbuks
and replaced them
with a single Crystal
and the purest sound
of an African Rattle
you could ever imagine.

And now it is like
an Old Hotel
managed by a nice man named "Hummercopf"

or something like that.
He has no truck with Obliquity
and he keeps my Deep Storage
all pleasantly organized and lit up
with the sheen of an Opal.
I draw my personal Presence
from the Black Box inside me
so it is as if I myself
were made of sweet Violets."

Alright alright. Enough about you.
Distribution cannot only be a Melee. I get that.
There is a certain Heredity
to the internal constitution of things
that is not oblique, but a
syzygetical doublet

surmounts the Globe
and gives it a spin
so all Confusion's particulates
become Great Circles
swirling to form a magnificent cosmic Presence
out of what once was Melee, merely.
Everything is quite comprehensible now.
Even Obliquity
has a history,
even Confusion
has its calculable distribution.
You just put the swarms and miasmas
into a fantastically ornamented metal cauldron and Melee
herself takes the form of your Syzygy.
You and me, babe,
will make a tour
of old Africa,
harness Happenstance,
have Heredity dance for us.
Jaguar be the center-piece,
Wrench Boy, white hunter,
Jaguar aloof on his ebony stallion.
Do they have stallions on that continent?
No matter.
There never were Violets at Black Lake
until we put them there, neither.
But magic stones
are ubiquitous if invisible.
Don't be confused by Hammerhead.
He has, in spite of it all,
Violets in his Heredity.
And whatever you think of the end of it,
it all will start all over again.

The Cryptographic Matrix

Views From Tornado Island has thirteen "books." I have chosen to publish "Book 12" first because I wanted to give the feel of an entire pass through what I call "the cryptographic matrix" and because, perhaps, it most completely represents the range and scope of the entire poem.

All thirteen deploy a matrix, and I am providing here a description of the procedure for its construction and use. Its presence as affecting the rhetorical play of the poem, the local structure of each section, its function in furthering or disrupting or otherwise conditioning the flow of the text, indeed its role in the poem's pretended "anagogy," will come in and out of pertinence for any given reader and for any given reading. One surely does not need to be familiar in detail with the "system" to undergo the poem. The systematic character of the composition is only a "subject" or "topic" of the poem along with all the other subjects and topics. In that respect, this is not a "procedural" or "systematic" poem at all. I present the procedure for the interested and the curious. That said, knowledge of it might indeed enhance or facilitate the working of the text.

The entire poem, as I say, is divided into thirteen "books," each book into a certain number of "sections." In many of the books, as in this one, there are precisely twenty-six of these, corresponding to the twenty-six letters of the English alphabet, each letter encoded by a word for an object, for an abstraction, for a proper name; in short, a "signifier." In addition to numbered sections, which are written with the use of the matrix, there are other unnumbered pieces called "intervals" which are composed without reference to the matrix. In some of the books the full alphabet of signifiers is not represented in all possible alphabetic positions; that is, there are less that twenty-six sections. What this means will become clear in a moment.

I use the two simplest forms of codes: a substitution code, where some signifier is substituted for each letter of the alphabet in a one-one fashion; a transposition code, where the substitution code is subjected to a further process under which each signifier is changed systematically (regarding its position in the series) to the position of another. I transpose the initial substitution one letter; that is, the signifier substituted for the letter "A" in one section is substituted for letter "B" in the next. Each section advances the code one letter. For example: In the first section of this book, the letter A is represented by "Wrench Boy," B by "Syzygy," Z by "Jaguar." Therefore, in second section, the letter A is "Jaguar," the letter B is "Wrench Boy," the letter C, "Syzygy."

The idea was not particularly to hide the message but to use these rudimentary cryptographic procedures to build a skeleton over which to incarnate my poem, or alternatively, to give myself a "skrying stone" or "magic mirror" (in the poem – a Rattle or an Opal) from which to conjure it.

For each book, an initial choice of twenty-six names, objects, and abstract qualities were selected and assigned arbitrarily to the twenty-six letters of the English alphabet. I now had a way of "writing out" a message as a series of encoding signifiers. Each book has a single phrase as its message and a unique choice of the twenty-six. The poem is conjured from the interaction of the message with its code.

The procedure for composition is as follows. I write out the title or (the message) of the book and substitute for its letters the assigned signifiers. I now compose freely according to the rule: the signifiers must appear in the order of their occurrence in the message. They may not appear except in the positions which that order prescribes. Language that goes between the signifiers is free. In effect, the poem comprises passages or bridges from one signifier to the next. Of course, that language is governed by the content that they suggest as I am writing; so, though I call them here for convenience "signifiers," their function is not particularly involved in technical linguistic notions: they are the characters, physical objects, abstract qualities and concepts they signify, and that to a very fluid and variable degree. The structure facilitates the invocation of connections between these things, beings, and notions, but also to interrupt the flow of thought or narrative that may have been developing at any given point and to allow for, as it were, thaumaturgic transformations at practically all levels of structure.

Once the message has been "encrypted"; that is, once the poem has developed through the series of signifiers assigned to the encrypted message, it is clear that only the signifiers substituting for the letters contained in the original message would be represented in the poem. In order to fill out the alphabet, I now solicit from the text that I have written words containing the letters not yet represented. I thus provide myself with new words to encode and proceed to substitute the appropriate signifiers for these new letters and to continue writing my poem as before. The section is complete as soon as I have used all the letters, A to Z.

Now I perform the first transposition, moving each signifier ahead one letter: what was "A" now is "B," "B" is now "C" and so forth. I repeat the entire compositional procedure until I have a complete rendering of the alphabet in this first transposed form. This will be the second section of the book.

I now transpose again and reiterate the transposition as many times as I wish—to generate, that is, as many sections as I sense belong to the book. With "Money Has An Enemy" (see the list of encrypted phrases at the end of this note for the messages of the thirteen books), when I had completed a set of twenty-six transpositions; i.e., when each signifier had appeared as each letter of the alphabet, I felt I had not at all exhausted what I wanted to do with this particular message, so I simply started again with the original distribution, went through the twenty-six transpositions again. When I had finished, again I felt that I had not finished. I completed four passes through the alphabetic transpositions, producing the first four books of the poem. As I remember, I actually stopped before the twenty-sixth transposition of *Money Has An Enemy, 4.*

Next I chose a new phrase. For the first four books after *Money Has An Enemy (5-8)* I did not go through the complete set of transpositions. But for the following four (9-12) I did do so, once for each book. The thirteenth book, the book from whose message the entire poem takes its title, once again, I did not complete the transpositions.

Liberality

As my experience with the system grew, I discovered that it was not necessary to deploy each element as a literal signifier: that is, I could use grammatical variants of the word in question, or occasionally substitute synonyms or closely related words. In "Book 12, " for "heredity" sometimes I use "inheritance" or "inherit." Also, in a few cases, I allow two different signifiers to occupy the same position and simply choose the one I want at each place. This occurs in the later Books of the poem and allows reiterations of and allusions to early books to occur in a formal way. Thus, in "Book 12," I give "ubiquity/absence" as a pair of possibilities, as well as "Long River/Deep Storage" and "distribute/disperse/dispossess." Occasionally, after I had finished composing, I discovered that I had made a mistake in setting up or composing from the matrix. Usually I simply accepted the mistake because the field integrity of the poem depended more upon what was actually written, than on the strenuousness with which I kept to the matrix. Therefore, if one tries to follow the code through a given text one might find such errors. But the point of the matrix was to generate the poem, not particularly to "reveal" the matrix as if it were its hidden meaning in some privileged way. There is at every point some relation between the manifest poem and its encrypted skeleton, but that is as variable as everything else in the poem.

Another caveat: I have for some of the sections made several compositional passes, intensifying, revising, elaborating, simplifying the text. I have tried to keep the correct order of the signifiers, but in some cases I may have erred and replaced them. I have not made a systematic check to discover where this is true. Also, once in a while, though I think quite rarely, I have simply revised the signifier away.

THE SIGNIFIERS FOR BOOK 12:

This is a list in order of the twenty-six signifiers in "Book 12" as used in the first section. Note that the titles of the sections are drawn from a feeling for the content of the section. Often they involved the dominant signifier of it, but not systematically so.

A: Wrench Boy
B: Syzygy
C: Violet
D: Hammerhead
E: Crystal / Stone
F: Melee
G: Black Lake
H: Black Box
I: African Rattle
J: Confusion
K: Opal
L: Nation
M: Globe / Glob
N: Old Hotel
O: Long River / Deep Storage
P: Ubiquity / Absence
Q: Incomprehensibility
R: Volatility
S: Stability (Stone)
T: Heredity
U: Dispossession / Distribution / Dispersion
V: Presence
W: Fragility
X: Strength
Y: Happenstance
Z: Jaguar

THE BEGINNING OF THE "MESSAGE," OF COURSE, IS THE WORD "THERE," WHICH, WITH THE SUBSTITUTIONS, LOOKS LIKE THIS:

T: Heredity
H: Black Box
E: Crystal
R: Volatility
E: Crystal

THE OPENING LINES OF THE FIRST SECTION ARE:

My **heredity**, I say,
is like a **black box —**
a **crystal**
in a cloud
above Tornado Island,
a **volatile** flux of sentient particulates
compressed in such a cloud as such a **Crystal.**

The Encoded Phrases for the Thirteen Books of *Views from Tornado Island* are these:

Book 1: Money Has An Enemy, 1
Book 2: Money Has an Enemy, 2
Book 3: Money Has an Enemy, 3
Book 4: Money Has an Enemy, 4
Book 5: Give Me a Lever and a Place to Stand
Book 6: The False Is The Form of The True
Book 7: A Lane to The Land of The Dead
Book 8: Across The Perilous Line
Book 9: The Mouse Eats Cat Food But The Cat's Bowl Is Broken
Book 10: Ploughing The Clouds
Book 11: Never Tire of The Road
Book 12: There Where You Do Not Think to Be Thinking
Book 13: Views from Tornado Island

The Drawings

From the beginning I made sketches of the "characters" (Jaguar, Hammerhead, Violet, and the others); I made images for the objects (African Rattle, Black Box, for instance) and drawings connected to abstractions, and other drawings I feel in some way linked to the poem. I continued to develop them throughout the process. "The Gallery of Images" is a collection of them.

www.ingramcontent.com/pod-product-compliance
Lightning Source LLC
Chambersburg PA
CBHW081740100526
44592CB00015B/2246
* 9 7 8 1 9 4 1 5 5 0 1 2 0 *